The Poet's Domain

The Poet's Domain

Collection of Poems

Volume Twenty-Five

Choose Something Like a Star

Compiled by Alexandria Tirrigan
Edited by Patricia S. Adler

Live Wire Press
www.livewirepress.net

Copyright © 2009 by Live Wire Press
Compiled by Alexandria Tirrigan
Edited by Patricia S. Adler

All rights reserved for one year from copyright date, including the right to reproduce this work in any form whatsoever, without permission in writing from the publisher, except for brief passages in connection with a review

Cover art: istockphoto.com

If you are unable to order this book from your local bookseller, you may order directly from the publisher.
padler@cstone.net or
www.livewirepress.net

ISBN for volume twenty-five: 978-0-9824490-0-4

Library of Congress Cataloging-in-Publication Data
She dwelt among the untrodden ways / compiled and edited by Patricia S. Adler.
   p. cm. -- (The poet's domain ; v. 17)
ISBN 0-9672885-2-5
   1. American poetry--20th century. 2. Wordsworth, William, 1770-1850 --Parodies, imitations, etc.   I. Adler, Patricia S., 1938-   . II. Series.
PS615.S448 2000
811'.508--dc21

00-010927

10 9 8 7 6 5 4 3 2 1
Printed in the United States

dedicated to
the tiniest star of all,

Madeline Grace Morton

cherished daughter of Mark and Karrie
much loved and dearly missed

Table of Contents

Editor's Note xiii

Sunday Abbott, *Virginia Beach, Va.*
Snow Storm 1

Patricia Adler, *Charlottesville, Va.*
Choose Something Like a Star 3

Don Amburgey, *Jenkins, Ky.*
Keystone 4

Jason Lester Atkins, *Virginia Beach, Va.*
Person of the Century 5

Dawn Bailiff, *Wilmington, Del.*
The Black Hole 7
Moon Child 8
Star Wars 9

Bartow H. Bridges Jr., *Virginia Beach, Va.*
Bridge 11
Haiku Quiet Scene 11
Haiku Temporary Gold 11
Haiku Music 12
Haiku Gone 12

Lilli Lee Buck, *Bristol, Va.*
The Lawyer and the Grim Reaper 13
The Apple Picker 17
Sir Thomas Moore 18
Silent Night 21
Abraham Lincoln's Prayer 23

Jack Callan, *Norfolk, Va.*
Chosen Bird 25

Elaine Cramer, *Hartly, Del.*
Over and Over 27
The Good Life 27
Letting Go 28
Out Staring 28

Anne Darrison, *Virginia Beach, Va.*
February Moon 29
Dreams 29
Common Language 29
Hope 30
apple trees 30

Mary F. Davis, *Rio Rancho, N.M.*
Te Deum of Tigra 31
Jean Doing, *Silver Spring, Md.*
Kalos 32
Resonance 33
Like Moths to a Star 34
An Out of Blues Experience 34
Music of a Country Poem 36
Terry Douglas, *Virginia Beach, Va.*
If I Could Paint 37
I Still Want to Dance 38
Where Are You? 39
Un-walled Spirit 40
Finger-Touch 41
Bea DuRette, *Hampton, Va.*
Homecoming 42
Spring Freeze 43
Parthenogen 44
The Last Room 45
Annunciation 46
Catherine Edwards, *Norfolk, Va.*
Quite Nicely 47
Margaret Edwards, *Charlottesville, Va.*
Nebula 48
Remorse 48
Pete Freas, *Chesapeake, Va.*
Nomads 49
Wheston Chancellor Grove, *Williamsburg, Va.*
Cat on Duke of Gloucester 51
Waiting The Sound of Aging 51
On Being Sophie Scholl 52
Doris Gwaltney, *Smithfield, Va.*
Water 53
William L. Hickey, *Virginia Beach, Va.*
Once and Future Buddies 54
Steven S. Hollberg, *Urbanna, Va.*
Flat Calm 56
Night Sail 57
Peggy Kelly, *Newport News, Va.*
Star 59

Robert L. Kelly, *Newport News, Va.*
Compass 60
Stabilization 60
Hotel Soap 61
Their Lodestar 62

Maddie Kline, *Woodside, Del.*
In Loving Memory of 63
Stardust 64
Heavensense 64

Barry M. Koplen, *Danville, Va.*
a hard one to read 65
dog-eared time 65
and you ask why 66
catfish 66

Margaret P. Latham, *Charlottesville, Va.*
After Winter Solstice 67
A Poet Reads from His Work 67
The Summer Person 68

Mary Antil Lederman, *Charlottesville, Va.*
Give Us This Day 69
Supernovas . . . Gone Too Soon 71
Not "In the Stars" 72
Etoile du Ballet 72
Tercet 73

Joseph Lewis, *Williamsburg, Va.*
Morning Stars 74
Listening to Bach 75

D. S. Lliteras, *Virginia Beach, Va.*
Prelude 76
Mortal 77

Edward W. Lull, *Williamsburg, Va.*
April One 78
The Limericker 78
For Sale by Bob 79

Betty Maistelman, *Virginia Beach, Va.*
Underwater Ballet 80

Mary L. Martin, *Chesapeake, Va.*
Stars on Earth 81
Synchronicity 82

Megan K. McDonald, *Fairfax, Va.*
In the Glass 83
Stepping Out of Shadows 84
Sunsets 84
Can a Shadow Be a Friend? 85
Moon Bath 86

Anne Meek, *Norfolk, Va.*
Amy Vanderbilt 87
Secret Funds 88
From Lisa's Porch 89
Shy 90
The Geneology of Raisin-Filled Cookies 91

Elaine Morgan, *Warrenton, Va.*
Piano Fingers 93
Still Point 94
Shaman on the Via Positiva 95

Lu Motley, *Richmond, Va.*
Sometimes during Summers 97
Teacher 98
To Frost 98

Ruby Lee Norris, *Topping, Va.*
Upon Viewing Albert Bierstadt's Mt. Corcoran 99
Upon Viewing Monet's Water Lilies 99
Through My Lens 100

Charlie Palumbo, *Gordonsville, Va.*
Cry 101
The Wilds of a Woman 102

Donna Harter Raab, *Fredreicksburg, Va.*
Wild Flower 103
The Tornado 104
The Water Answers 105

Robert A. Rickard, *Northern Neck, Va.*
Choosing Light 107

Dawn Riddle, *Smithfield, Va.*
The Companions 109

Tom Russell, *Harrisonburg, Va.*
Erasmus Darwin's Grandson 110
St. Francis, Perfection 110

Lynn Veach Sadler, *Sanford, N.C.*
Fears Allayed 111
Lemurs and Other Spirits 111
Guideposts 112
Here's to the New Philistines 114

Lynda Self, *Waynesville, N.C.*
The Promise Recanted 116
Late Summer 117

Shirley Nesbit Sellers, *Norfolk, Va.*
December Windows 118
Starlight 118
Wartime Goodbye 119

Ann Falcone Shalaski, *Newport News, Va.*
Center of the Universe 120
Falling Back into Life 121
Hope 121
Family Matters 122

Barbara Drucker Smith, *Newport News, Va.*
While Dancing 123

George Stietz, *Gloucester, Va.*
Lila 124

H. Anne Stratford, *Scranton, Pa.*
Constellation 125
sunset haiku 125
Orison 126

Mary Talley, *Virginia Beach, Va.*
When I Lose Count 127

Lesley M. Tyson, *Reston, Va.*
question a star 128
control the night 128
something like a star 129
star-crossed 129
hope upon a star 130

Jack Underhill, *Falls Church, Va.*
The Miracle of Birth 131
An Ominous Black Hole in the Sky 132

Elizabeth Urquhart, *Hampton, Va.*
Waiting for the Foxes 134
Geronimo 135
Cinco de Mayo 136
The Navajo Code Talkers 136
Sara Swifthawk 138

Douglas Alan Wandersee, *Harrisonburg, Va.*
The Properties of Tapioca 140

The Poet's Domain

Edith White, *Norfolk, Va.*
Looking Up 141
Stardust Universe 142
An Evening in May 143
Preserves 144

Louise B. Wilson, *Virginia Beach, Va.*
Beauty 145
Waiting New Life 145

Robert E. Young, *Virginia Beach, Va.*
evermore 146
Vincent's Bedroom at Arles, 1888 146
Advice: The Lost and the Found 147
Rheumy 148

Steven Zimmerman, *Fort Wayne, Ind.*
Being Not Doing 149
Ethereal Friend 149
Plucking Comets 150

Rabbi Israel Zoberman, *Virginia Beach, Va.*
A Starbucks' Moment 151
Flight's Joy 151
Hanan, My Iraqi Sister 151
Mirror's Magic 152
Virginia Beach 152

Choose Something Like a Star

Editor's Note

Dear Poets,

    I thank you once again for your trust in sharing your hearts and work. Although the poems in this volume embody a wide range of interpretation—I like to call it a kaleidoscope of perspectives—I believe the theme itself, as it relates to Frost's admonition, has great value in turbulent times.

    Each of us needs to find in our own heart, a quiet peaceful place of refuge—a place to renew our faith and values—where we meet our truth and come away refreshed and confident. This wellspring enables us to create our lives with passion and move forward with courage.

    It is my pleasure to present volume twenty-five.

Pat Adler

Choose Something Like a Star

Snow Storm

By the time I reach
the apple tree
on the far side of the field

the sparse, lazy snow
has grown thick and fast
on a shifting wind blowing it
in wide, blinding swirls

that turn me around until
I don't know which way
to head for home and cling
fearfully to the old, arthritic tree
so serenely anchored there.

Of course, the tree doesn't count time, afraid
of being caught with night coming on.
Of course, it doesn't worry about being lost—
it's already home—

but there's comfort in the way
it allows the storm to unfold,

the way it stands by me, our edges blurred
with those of fences and posts, foxes and crows,

in the storm's smoky whiteness and falling snow,
its tissue-thin wings whispering and humming
like a buzz of electric voices
hidden in wires on telephone poles.

Sunday Abbott lives with her lovely daughter in Virginia Beach, Virginia where she hopes to adopt the lifestyle of their five Zen cats, who care naught for fame or pedigree but eat when hungry, nap when sleepy, play when frisky, and live contentedly *in the meow.*

The Poet's Domain

Sunday Abbott

Sound fills the hollows of my skull
runs the edges of my bones
so that I too am their song
and by now, having lost all notion of
singularity
or being set apart from the weather,

I fling my bony branches out
and gather blossoms of snow
content to simply bloom

as the tree does each spring
performing on cue, its
fresh, pale petals

like lips blowing
kisses
to an audience of bees.

Choose Something Like a Star

When the heart needs
something to hold on to—
an anchor to cling to—
a safe place to regain peace—
I'd like to choose a star
as Frost advises,
but I find them, first of all,
too far away.
I'd rather something to look at,
feel, hold, or touch—
you can't always see the stars—
undoubtedly human frailty
on my part.
I sought advice and was told
to speak to trees.
Out loud.
Okay.
I've done worse.
I found three trees,
planted in a triangle.
I stood in the middle
and spoke my heart.
They said I was the first person
to speak to them.
They took my tale and carried it home.

They are black locust I found,
the bark of which is used
herbally as a cathartic;
metaphorically—letting go.

The city has decided
to down these trees
to make the street wider.

Maybe a star . . .

Patricia Adler

is a native of New Jersey, and has lived in Virginia for twenty-six years. Language and linguistics have been consistent themes in her life in tandem with art and music. Pat was a teacher for eighteen years and has a masters in French from George Mason University where she also taught in the late eighties. She has been working in the publishing field for the past twelve.

The Poet's Domain

Don Amburgey

is a teacher, drama producer, and a regional librarian in Kentucky. Numbered among his pastimes are: the love of music and storytelling; playing banjo, guitar, and mandolin. However, reading remains his dominant pleasure. His writings include poetry, stories, and a fictionalized biography: *Constantine Samuel Rafinesque, Solo Naturalist*. With wife, Joyce, a librarian, he lives in Jenkins, Kentucky.

Keystone

My astonishment! On first reading the
canyon walls
Along highway 23!

Rock layers, each a million years in making,
Eras upthrusting, forming new leaves for the
book . . .
The earth billions of years rounding out from
Inner gravity . . . my corporeal body, too,
Accreted, cell by cell, from an inner gravity.

I return to dust and scatter in the wind;
Rock strata crumble to grit dissolving each
leaf,
Washing away to sea grain by grain;
The globe will vaporize, dispersing us to the
universe . . .
Again . . . stuff for new stars.

But, how exhilarating my flash of life has been,
Like a brief suspension, between the darkness
Of two eternities!

Choose Something Like a Star

Person of the Century
Time Magazine's naming
Albert Einstein the
"Person of the Century."

Riding on a beam of speeding light
flashing out among our spirit gatherings,
Albert's knowing energy of compassion flows:
knowing life is a photograph of the brain:
knowing his brain stolen by Princeton
pathologist:
flashing picture wisdoms from a stationary time
before he was all mustache and wrinkles:

zapping, a million years into eternity's second:
teaching we are but temporary consuming
guests
on our whirling ball of blue mud called earth:
waiting for our next contrived millennium:
waiting for our next constructed apocalypses:
consuming sixty million years of dinosaur's
blood:
consuming trees and plants creating air:

asking, how many earths surround two
billion stars:
knowing spirit and knowledge evolve
clutching strong impulses from our primitive
pasts:

Jason Lester Atkins

was born in Hampton, Va., attended Huntington School of Engineering, and the University of Oklahoma. He was a gunner on a torpedo bomber in WW II. His first published story appeared in *Holiday* magazine in 1950. His published poetry has appeared in *The Poet's Domain, Borders, Writer's Voice, Beacon,* and *West Virginia Review*. He is now retired and is facilitator of the Virginia Beach Writer's Group.

The Poet's Domain

Jason Lester Atkins

seeing last millennium a child of physics:
seeing new millennium a child of biology:
knowing we must lift the veil on smallest things,
discovering quantums of light on the back of a mouse:

knowing, roads to enlightenment are not star voyages
disturbing old beliefs that prevent love:
learning,
"Science without religion is lame:
Religion without science is blind:"
placing gold crowns and silver robes on Priests
surrenders love's power to a passing artifact:
surrenders power of what we make of God.

The Black Hole

Rules of nature that confine and bind
when all I want is to be friends.

The caged bird sings inside my broken ribs,
ripping through the fat
that I have earned—
the fat that now protects me
from the stares of men.

Painful flashback:
those stares once led to Heaven—once . . .
when I believed.

Now, without the strength to climb,
I am forced to fly,
revealing my scabby wings for all to see.
Yet, that is how God made me.

Indeed, my wings spread easily now,
that the middle years have weakened my
resolve
to be grounded.

Better to be a broken bird
than a sprightly snake.
It is too difficult to gain respect
with your face slithering in the dirt—
no matter how good you feel.

These hand-me-down wings do not quite fit:
I am again a little girl, trying . . .
trying on her mother's shoes,
but, at least, wings make high heels redundant.

Dawn Bailiff

A former concert pianist, Dawn is a published author and translator, whose poetry and short fiction appears frequently in periodicals and anthologies such as *The Poet's Domain.*

The Poet's Domain

Dawn Bailiff

Moon Child

I would crawl inside the moon,
Wrapped in shawl of shadows

To view the earth from silver tomb—
A life encased, no promised birth
To mar the safe, smooth womb.

Would I feel the pains and fears
Of those beneath my gaze;
Would passing minutes . . .
Hours . . . Years
Become one night's blue haze?

To me it seems the transient earth would fall
away in time

A planet paled by satellite,
As Poet Lost to Rhyme.

Age-taught confines seem large in light,
Grow dim as darkness falls:

Vision can't teach us to see
Through daytime practicality
There's death in sunlight's walls.

But play and dreams are born again as darkness cradles Mars.

Moonbeams shout.
The child within
Stands tall against the stars.

Dawn Bailiff

Star Wars

"I love you more than all the stars."
What does it mean without
wiping the vomit,
crying the tears,
taking the car to the mechanic?

If words were needs would they ever be enough
to transport you across these miles of
anguish into my aching bed?

Years of arguments have left me old but not
too wise,
warping the dense ball of feelings in my chest,
bouncing higher, higher until it beats within
my mind
like an angry game of racquetball.

Will the shards of the girl you once "loved"
be enough
for you to love
when you are man enough to love
the woman in me . . . if
you ever grow into a man?
And if your "manhood" remains confined to
games of war and toys of death,
why would I want you? . . . Why, indeed?
Could it be that I've been playing, too?

With purposes, legs, and fingers crossed,
I play at being young,
while you play a grown-up.
Yet, games are no fun
when the outcome is assured:

The Poet's Domain

Dawn Bailiff

soon pushed from the winner's pedestal,
I will be forced to see the stars
for what they really are.

It is so difficult to appear graceful
in a broken heel, and yet, I must stand tall.

After all:

I bled before the knives,
cried before the pain,
yearned before the sex,
cringed in fear before . . .
the death.

War is not just for boys.

Choose Something Like a Star

Bridge

Nature set the stage
Water, beach, trees, meadow.
Then brushed in
Fog, chill, dampness, quiet;

But with human influences—
Dark steel structures,
Vertical and horizontal;
Massive but functional.

Gloomy in the fog from below.
But different from above.
Functional, majestic, beautiful, busy;
When sun lit, the Golden Gate Bridge.

Haiku
Quiet Scene

Moonlight on water.
Ripples shatter the image,
Why does moon scatter?

Haiku
Temporary Gold

Gingko waits for fall
Then leaves become golden gems
Only for a few days.

Bartow H. Bridges Jr.

(aka "Pat" Bridges), born 1928, is a native of Virginia Beach, Va. After graduating from the University of Maryland he was a landscape nurseryman for fifteen years, then an instructor of horticulture and landscape design for seven years, then a self-employed landscape architect and horticulture consultant for twenty-seven years. Now semi-retired, he lives with his wife, Betty, in Atlantic Shores Retirement Community in Virginia Beach where he is a member of a writers' group.

Bartow H. Bridges Jr.

Haiku
Music

Sudden gust of wind
Sweeps through branches and marsh grass.
Silent symphony.

Haiku
Gone

Flower petal falls—
Lands softly in mountain stream;
Then flows out of sight.

Choose Something Like a Star

The Lawyer and the Grim Reaper

The Grim Reaper and the Devil went strolling one night,
Seeking someone who was not well.
The Grim Reaper wanted to take someone's life.
The Devil wanted a soul for Hell.

Mr. Blaine had been practicing law,
For thirty-five years so far,
At the District Court, the Circuit Court,
And even the Supreme Court bar.

He had fought for his dear country,
With valor in the Great War.
Now he served his God in peacetime,
To study war no more.

His wife had died five years before.
His children had moved away.
And the old man was lonely every night and day,
And longed for love in vain.

Old age had brought arthritis,
And arthritis brought him pain.
And he limped when he walked and softly moaned,
As he leaned upon his cane.

But he wanted to keep on living,
As most living people do.
And he tried to serve God every day,
And prayed God to bring him through.

Lilli Lee Buck

born Feb. 25, 1950, in Butler, Pennsylvania, now lives in Bristol, Va. Lilli has published poetry since 1980. From a family of writers, her grandfather, Cephas Shelburne Buck, and uncle, Cephas Crockett Buck, both published books of poetry, in 1924 and 1979 respectively. Lilli graduated from the College of William and Mary, with a B.A. in 1972, and an M. Ed. in 1984. A former teacher, she now lives on a small farm, where she has an animal shelter, and works for animal and human rights, and environmental causes.

The Poet's Domain

Lilli Lee Buck

But the Grim Reaper came a-knocking,
One night for this old man.
Said Death, "I'll carry you away.
Defeat me if you can."

Mr. Blaine said, "I'll defeat you, Death,
Upon this very night.
It's unlawful for you to take my life,
According to the Bill of Rights."

"You can't escape me when I stalk.
I'll still your tongue so you can't talk."
"Well, the First Amendment guarantees
That I have Freedom of Speech.

So you have no right to still my tongue
So that I can't talk or teach."
"I'll steal your soul so you can't pray.
When I command you must obey."

"Oh, no, it is illegal
For you to steal my soul from me.
For I have Freedom of Religion,
The First Amendment granted me."

"I'll close your eyes 'til you are blind.
Your worldly goods you must leave behind.
In your stately home you cannot stay.
Strange men will carry you away."

"Oh, no, it is unlawful
For you to steal my goods from me,
Or for you to take me from my home,
Deprived of liberty.

Lilli Lee Buck

"For you can't take my life, liberty, or property
Without due process of law.
Thus states the Fifth Amendment.
Thus cruel death has been outlawed.

"And you cannot arrest or jail me,
For I have done no crime.
According to the Writ of Habeas Corpus,
And this is not my time."

The Grim Reaper scratched his bony head.
He was a mite perplexed,
Wondering what tricks that foxy lawyer
Would play upon him next.

"But you are old and lonely,
You are crippled, you are lame.
What have you got to live for,
When your life is fraught with pain?"

He said, "I wake up every morning,
When the Daystar rises bright,
And see the green, green leaves of summer
Sparkling in the sunlight.

"All God's creatures are rejoicing,
And the songbirds sing to me.
I breathe the cool fresh country air.
Oh, Death, depart from me."

Quoth he, "I live to serve my God,
And when He calls me home,
Then I will go quite willingly,
No more on earth to roam.

Lilli Lee Buck

"But you have no right to take my life
From me against my will.
Christ is my Lord and you are not.
He can heal and He can kill.

"And I will sue you in Federal Court
If you deprive me of my life.
I can sue you, I'm a lawyer.
That is my Sixth Amendment right.

"And you will go to prison
If you steal my life from me.
There may you lurk among the criminals,
But let the righteous man go free.

"And death, I declare, is a cruel,
If not unusual, punishment,
Banned by the Eighth Amendment,
With all other forms of torment.

"Therefore, Death, it is illegal
For you to take my life tonight.
You have no jurisprudence here,
For I am living right."

So cold, black Death, he turned away,
And left that man alive and well.
Said the Devil, "I don't want that man
To confound us down in Hell."

"So let's find some hardened criminal,
Whose soul has not been saved.
I'll take his soul with me to Hell,
And you can lay him in his grave."

Lilli Lee Buck

The Apple Picker

She came to pick the apples from his tree.
The sunlight dancing on the apple leaves
Cast dappled shade upon the grass.
The sunlight glistened golden on her long hair,
And the breeze blowing through the apple tree
Rustled as it passed.

The sunshine reddened the apples in her young cheeks,
And her skin was smooth as velvet,
As velvet as the moss.
Her body was as lissome as the apple boughs.
She rubbed an apple on her shirt,
And polished it to a gloss.

He knew that he was much too old to love her,
And that if he should tell her, she might think it a disgrace.
But she could hear the love tones in his old voice.
She saw the love light in his eyes,
And saw the softness in his face.

He said, "Take all the apples you can carry.
Go home and make some applesauce
Or bake an apple pie."
He knew he was too old for her to marry,
But oh! She was the apple of his eye!

Love sometimes comes where it is least expected.
Sometimes love comes unbidden. Sometimes it comes unknown.
Sometimes love stays hidden. Sometimes it is rejected,
But love still shines with tender beauty,
Even when it shines alone.

The Poet's Domain

Lilli Lee Buck

Sir Thomas Moore

King Henry and Queen Catherine
Had been married for many a year,
But when Catherine got old and past her prime,
Henry wanted rid of her.

So he looked over her ladies-in-waiting,
And he fancied Anne Boleyn,
But though he chased her and embraced her,
She would not yield to him.

"Nay, nay, nay, nay," quoth Anne Boleyn,
"Not until I am your queen.
I will not be your light leman,
Though you give me sleeves of green."

"Nay, nay, nay, nay," quoth Anne Boleyn,
"Not until I am your wife."
How little did she think back then
That to be Queen would cost her life.

Henry sent a request to the Pope in Rome
For a divorce from his aging Queen.
"Nay, nay, nay, nay," quoth the Pope in Rome.
Henry waxed wroth with spleen,

Saying, "The Pope hath none authority
Over what I do in my own realm.
I will make a new church, the Church of England,
And only I will be at its helm."
They've written up an oath on pain of death,
That all the courtiers must sign,
Saying that the Pope had no authority in England,
And Queen Anne's children would succeed in line.

Choose Something Like a Star

Lilli Lee Buck

The dukes and earls and ministers
All took the oath and swore,
For they sought King Henry's favor,
All except Sir Thomas Moore.

Thomas Moore, the Lord High Chancellor,
Held out, refused to sign.
"Take the oath! Take the oath," they urged him,
But from his high office he resigned.

So they clamped him in the Tower,
And they stripped him of his rights.
They clapped him in a dank, dark cell,
Shut up with rats and mice.

"I'll find a way," King Henry said,
"To cut off this traitor's head.
I'll have no opposition.
The man's as good as dead."

Sir Thomas, he stayed silent.
He would not tell them why,
For if he should speak against the King,
He knew he'd have to die.

His daughter came to see him,
Saying, "Father, take the oath.
We are desolate without you,
And to lose you we are loath."

"Nay, nay, nay, nay," quoth Sir Thomas Moore,
Who took a moral stand,
"For I never will forswear myself
For the sake of any man."

Lilli Lee Buck

So they made up false charges against him,
And took him to a trumped-up trial,
Where they condemned this righteous man to death,
By perjury and guile.

Sir Thomas, he addressed the court,
When he knew he was condemned,
Saying, "Now I shall discharge my mind,
Though I never speak again.

"When Jesus Christ was here on earth,
Alive and in the flesh,
He chose St. Peter to build his church,
And Peter's Holy See was blessed.

"And every Pope that followed him,
Is in St. Peter's line,
And becomes the Vicar of Jesus Christ,
Up to the present time.

"Therefore hath the Pope the power,
That no king may now usurp.
The Pope holds God's authority
Over every king on earth."

Sir Thomas Moore stood at the block,
About the hour of nine,
Saying, "Axe man, axe man, shudder not
To take this life of mine,

"For you send me straight to Heaven,
Without regret or rue,
For I never have sworn falsely,
And to my God I have been true."

Choose Something Like a Star

Lilli Lee Buck

Silent Night
France, the Western Front,
Dec. 25, 1914

Snow upon the twisted barbed wire.
Was it for this our Lord was born?
Snow in muddy, bloody trenches,
Where soldiers live and die forlorn.

Those men across the No-Man's Land,
They tell us they're the enemy,
And so we have to kill them,
People that we never see.

Christmas Eve, and what's the use of it?
Was it for this our Savior died,
To save mankind from all our sins?
Now in the trenches we abide.

Fire, bullets, bombs, explosions.
When will it ever stop?
And all too soon they'll give the order,
That we must go "over the top."

I wish I were back home with my mother,
Eating plum pudding and Shepherd's Pie,
Singing carols around the hearth fire.
Into her arms I long to fly.

What is that across the No-Man's Land?
It is a song that we all know.
The Germans are singing "Silent Night,"
In the trenches, in the snow.

"Silent Night"—I'll sing along with them.
After all, it's Christmas Eve.
Christ was born to bring us peace on earth,
He told us "Love your enemies."

The Poet's Domain

Lilli Lee Buck

Soon British voices joined the Germans,
In singing that holy song.
And the guns and bombs fell silent,
As everybody sang along.

After that, across the No-Man's Land,
White flags of truce were soon upraised,
For their hard hearts had been softened
By the singing of God's praise.

Soldiers swarmed into the No-Man's Land,
And their guns lay on the ground,
And except for songs and friendly greetings,
Silence reigned for miles around.

They shook hands with one another,
And treated the foe as friends.
They shared food, and showed family pictures,
As if the war were at an end.

For one day they observed the Peace of God.
Jesus was the Prince of Peace.
It was "all quiet along the Western front."
For one day the killing ceased.

Willie, Wilhelm, Henry, Heinrich,
Jacob, James, Johann, and John
Sang and worshipped God together
Until Christmas Day was past and gone.

But the warlords said, "This will not do.
What we need is fear and hate.
We can't let them love their enemies,
Or let hostilities abate."

So Colin said goodbye to Fritz,
And said, "Farewell, old mate.
Maybe when the war is over,
If we both escape a bullet's fate,

Lilli Lee Buck

"We'll go into a pub somewhere,
And I'll buy you a beer,
And we'll sing 'Silent Night' together,
And remember Christmas here."

Then the music of the Devil,
The sound of guns and shells and bombs,
Replaced the music of the Lord,
And the cruel war continued on.

Abraham Lincoln's Prayer

In a forest with no roads, only Indian trails,
I was born on a bed made of sapling rails,
In a little log cabin with just a dirt floor,
But I didn't know that we were poor.

On a corn husk mattress I took my rest.
Sometimes a humble bed is best,
For Christ was born on a bed of straw,
When the ox and lamb looked on and saw.

As a child I worked in the fields all day.
I never had much time to play,
I got up at the crack of morn,
For splitting rails and hoeing corn.

But by very hard work a man is made.
Christ himself worked at the carpenter's trade.
The Bible was the only book we had,
When I was just a little lad.

So after supper every night,
I read the Good Book by the firelight.
I prayed, "Lord, let me be like you.
Let my heart be righteous, kind, and true.

The Poet's Domain

Lilli Lee Buck

"I can't raise the dead or heal the blind,
But some holy purpose help me find."
God had a mission planned for me,
To set the slaves in bondage free.

It was on Good Friday that I died,
Like Christ, around the Easter tide.
Jesus Christ died upon a tree.
A bullet was the death of me.

If for sinners Christ gave his perfect life,
Then but little was my sacrifice,
For I was a sinner like all the rest,
But with a righteous mission I was blessed.

Choose Something Like a Star

Chosen Bird

Once, long ago
near Lao Chun Temple
on a quiet night
before memory could fade
Hsuah-Tsung was told in a dream
that semen from the great
white star Venus
had fallen to earth transforming
itself into a huge white boulder
deep within the sacred mountains of China
where only hermits dwelt.
With great difficulty and
without a path to follow
he found it and with reverence
had it carved into a statue
of Lao Tsu.
Here now is what happened:
the chosen bird that flew across
the night sky of heaven-scented universe
has tango danced, thigh thrown
over bent knee of love's warm arousal
takes two steps back and lets leg slip
between star sack of jewels clenched
tightly for leap of delight.
The fabric of skirt is lifted to feel
the back of thigh as wet heat transforms
itself into a chosen star in ecstasy.
There is a home beneath this altar
many stars away as love is
dripped across the Milky Way
to a far-flung shoulder hung
with suckling child to a small nest
like a lap to dream on
coming up for air

Jack Callan

Oldest of seven siblings, a hippy born to a Navy fighter pilot, Jack Callan became a carpenter and builder for thirty years. More recently he found himself an artist out of control. His work has been frequently on display at several locations around Hampton Roads. About six years ago Jack fell in with a number of area poets and writers, and has since been unable to stop writing despite the best efforts of his doctor.

The Poet's Domain

Jack Callan

to a dream befitting the messenger who
knows the sacred path through darkness
where effort need not be expended
the going only the getting
and getting home feels so abundant.
The piano player has left the room
the dancers' shoes are strewn about
with laces soaked in blood
the evidence of the ten thousand things
the day before night began before day
the bird of heaven at rest
a silence beyond the sanctity
with horses no longer bred for war
when the Tao is present
in the universe
when the sky alone
will be dark enough
to see this.

Over and Over

The poles we wrap
our lives around
break in sudden wind.
Vines scattered underfoot
grope blindly
for new ways to stand.
Over and over.

The Good Life

I tied the good life on a string
and flew it like a kite.
It surged ahead on frothy gusts
and dwindled out of sight.

I hooked the good life like a fish.
It dragged me, boat and all,
through deserts of salt water
where raindrops did not fall.

I chased it over dunes of time.
It burrowed in the sand.
I fell before the scale of years
with upturned, empty hands.

My legs are lean and muscled
from miles that I have run.
I dread the crown of weariness
that waits me when I'm done.

The good life never rested.
It never let me play.
Perhaps I tried too hard to win
myself an easy way.

Elaine Cramer

(born 1953, Baltimore, Maryland) graduated from Drew University with a degree in anthropology. As a systems analyst, Elaine spent many years writing for computers but has traded her lines of "code" for verse. She resides in Wyoming, Delaware, with a cat and itinerant birds. Her poems appeared in volumes 19–24 of *The Poet's Domain*.

Elaine Cramer

Letting Go

Long clenched, the rock
crumbled in my hand.
My heart stopped,
frantic fingers grabbing
air. Suspended there,
I found in nothing something
unbreakable.

Out Staring

The stars at a glance did level me
And as I did not rise but stared
They seized the game and gazed at me.
Eyes met mine without a blink.
The glistening orbs amassed like ants
Across a prostrate body raced
From shoes to forehead, tickling feet
The touch so light that I could feel them
Only when I dimmed my sight.

Laughing then, I claimed defeat
And rose to walk on through the night.

Choose Something Like a Star

February Moon

Lo! The ice pale February moon
scarves of clouds across her face
serene, round glides across the sky

She admires her progress in the lake
cold, motionless, a shining mirror
reflecting back her light, betraying

Two lovers in the shadows

Dreams

and the sun is rising already
no-one said we would be here forever
or tomorrow either, just so happens
like much of our lives, unplanned
an end to end cycle, foregone conclusion
one ant trailing its meandering path
inconsequential in its minute size
patiently carrying grain upon grain
building dreams to the stars.

Common Language

Silk with strength of steel
Bamboo swaying in the wind
Pliant bodies that must bend
Eyes behind shuttered veils

Quiet eyes that own the world
Inner fortress never scaled
One common language all
The daily lives of woman

Anne Darrison

is the poetic voice of Anne Morgan. Raised in Needham, Mass., Anne graduated from Case-Western Reserve University in Ohio, and eventually settled in California. There she was employed as a clinical medical technologist in research laboratories and hospitals. She studied Spanish literature and traveled with her daughter in Spain and Mexico. She retired in 1999 due to brain surgery. Anne writes poetry, short stories, and humorous articles.

Anne Darrison

Hope

Next year, there must be hope
for one more year, just one
One sheaf to prove a crop
seeds for next year's harvest

One soldier returns from war
plows the blood of his comrades
into green crops over shrapnel
healing his and earth's wounds

One child survives starvation
seed of life's next generation
new growth from tainted ground
Spring of new beginnings

and there will be Hope

apple trees

Ah, the apple trees! The distant memory
of a crisp spring morning temptation
for a wayward, wandering school girl
to stray midst fragrant forbidden paths

Under the sunlit blossom canopy
whirling, fingertips just touching
fairy skirts in pink and white lace
wind lightly tossing their petticoats

Given Wind's gentle benediction
Tousle haired, apple petal crowned
the village changeling elf child
late to duty, danced on her way

Choose Something Like a Star

Te Deum of Tigra

Oh Lovely Lord,
The Leaves are dancing
To the warm bright Earth.
I delight in the day
You have given me
To dream away.
The night is my palace,
Glittering in abundance.

I behold your gifts
In amazement
And joy,
As I prance
In your scented evening
Beneath the sky
Of orange blossoms,
Among the diamond
Fireflies,
With the wholeness
Of life,
Limber in my
Beating body,
Before I tremble
Into the winter ground.

I pat your Bless'ed Face
With my strip'ed paw,
For I am your beloved Beast,
Still stalking butterflies,
But just in play—
I pray!

Mary F. Davis

was born in Colorado and grew up in New Mexico. She is a graduate of the Writer's Workshop of the University of Iowa and continues to write poetry and prose. She has a daughter and two sons and resides in New Mexico with one of her sons. At one time she found homes for homeless animals and still is an animal advocate. She is a member of The Poetry Society of Virginia.

The Poet's Domain

Jean Doing

is an active member of the Writers' Center, Bethesda, Maryland and a graduate of the College of William and Mary. Retired human resource executive, Jean works as part-time director of a nonprofit that provides job counseling for people fifty-five and older, and has been published in *Scribble* magazine (Maryland writers) and *LitWit*, a Washington, D.C. humor periodical. Her work was included in two anthologies: *The Poet's Domain* and *Oasis Journal*, 2006, 2007, and 2008 and was accepted for *New England Poetry Journal*, 2008. Jean published a first collection/chapbook entitled *Catch the Sun* in 2007.

Kalos

You left
in a cloud of whale dandruff
spewing frosty spray
like the bow of a catboat
tacking in a wintry channel
pushed by January wind.

I stayed indoors
by the fire
turning my kaleidoscope
this way and that
to gain perspective
find a pattern
a color clue,
some reflective symmetry
from the glass and mirror.
My efforts brought only bursting lights
twisted patterns
and frozen tears.

A sensible person knows
whales have no dandruff.
Still I twist the kaleidoscope
hoping the optic tube will yield
one brilliant image
of our life together,
before tumbling the sparkling fragments
forward to infinity.

Choose Something Like a Star

Jean Doing

Resonance

At the Library of Congress the poet with a
shock of white hair
and wearing a tweed jacket
read his verse aloud
sharing fragments of his life.

I heard the quality of his voice
and cadence of his speech
steeped by nine generations of New Englanders
fueled by his California birth and boyhood
tempered by his love of plants and flowers
disciplined by his poor showing as a farmer
and early problems as family provider.
Robert Frost lived out his "lovers' quarrel"
with the world.

He crafted verse
mesmerized city dwellers like me.
Though the poet stopped speaking
we echo his one liners
hang onto his phrases and foibles.
We see peaceful traditions in Frost
despite darkness and rural hardship.

From this poet I know
of the "road not taken"
that we all seek answers
and like the children in California
"we all must eat our peck of gold,"
choosing "something like a star
to stay our minds on and be staid."

The Poet's Domain

Jean Doing

Like Moths to a Star

Dreams fall from the moon
weaving through stars
floating down lightly
touching earth
near the loom of our lives.

Wishes woven into tapestry
providing luster and intensity
or simply more fabric
when we woolgather
or fail to heed
their heavenly messages.

Wise to keep our hands busy
with the back and forth rhythm
of the shuttle on the loom
eyes lifted
towards heaven
hoping to be drawn
like moths to a star.

An Out of Blues Experience

Clouds of smoky chiffon
drifted across from Alexandria
hovered over Hains Point
changing golfers and bikers
to ethereal puppets.
Fog pushed under Memorial Bridge
billowed blanket-like
around the Kennedy Center cluster
settled stubbornly for the day,
a raincoat on the river.

Jean Doing

Evening was about fog and obscurity,
a large mass of water vapor
condensed to fine particles
above Washington.
Concert goers and theatre patrons
fog-bound and frustrated by traffic,
uncertain—not able to see clearly.
At Kennedy Center intermission
those who dared to step outside
to walk on the promenade,
turned their backs on bright lights,
the stroll and be seen security
of the inside lobby.

From Georgetown's Blues Alley
a few notes from a bass artist
got loose, drifted in the fog
towards the Potomac
and were experienced
as throbbing, dark chords
brilliant and clear,
from the deepest viol of all.
Only the handful on the Kennedy Terrace
caught William Parker's magic sound
as it blew away the raincoat on the river,
sailed toward the stars
carrying a celestial song,
from an earthbound city.

The Poet's Domain

Jean Doing

Music of a Country Poem

Softness of green moss
whispered motion over golden grasses
chords from a Spanish guitar,
metered, building,
turning in a circle
to begin again.
Sounds to explore
woodlands, rustic places
trying to catch a butterfly
with a paper cup.
You can't risk crushing its wings.
You stand aside
yielding space.
The song vanishes
before your heart
can close around it.

Choose Something Like a Star

If I Could Paint

If I could paint,
I'd walk across
The aqua sea,
Step over ripple waves,
Allow cerise reflection
To dry untouched.

I'd pass cormorants
Dancing tip-toe intricate
Before plunging deep;
Catch welcome on a breeze,
As I'd hasten to this canvas
Stretched horizon wide.

I'd feel chill-toe splash
To reach before scarlet
Burst amidst magnolia clouds,
Sketched rough in haste
In gray dawn light,
When all was quiet still.

Once there touch-close
I'd estimate his texture,
Movement—depth—swirl,
The artistry contained therein
That drew me close from
Far out beyond the sands.

And in this private showing
I'd ponder his intent and
In his purpose add
Buff lines—dimension,
Suggesting shape—direction
To this blossoming dawn.

Terry Douglas resumed writing poetry after his wife of thirty-nine years passed on five years ago. He was raised in New York City and attended university there. Following his entry into the CIA, he resided abroad in Warsaw, New Delhi, Beirut, and Berlin before returning to Virginia with his wife and five children. In addition to *Rules for Engaging Grief: A Path to Healing* and two volumes of poetry, he is awaiting publication of *Praying Fingertips*, a collection of his daily meditations, by Holy Fire Publishing.

Terry Douglas

I Still Want to Dance

I still want to dance,
Though you think
I've forgotten steps,
Never caught them.

I still want to explore,
Discover learn engage
Listen to plights and joys
Serve in love's capacity.

I still want to share
Your adventures
Even if mind limited,
Extend heart boundaries.

I still want to love
You near and far,
Share sunsets,
Quiet moments 'til dawn.

I still want to laugh,
Parse joy solace,
Offer encouragement,
Boundless enthusiasm.

I still want to dance.

Terry Douglas

Where Are You?

At times you linger
Beside me on the right,
Whispering sometime shouting
Through mind-heart clamor.

Outside of me you conjure
Yesterday's regrets
Stirring aflame memories,
As if to rewind reality.

Observing—witnessing
You know me intimately,
Yet you prefer it seems
To remain apart.

And I reluctant become
Your object examined
From afar through time
Caught in past neglects;

That is until I reach across,
Outside myself to you,
Grip you close tight and pull
So we two become one.

In present time—no past,
We see vision clear,
Gain perspective even wisdom
For what is unfolding now.

Terry Douglas

Un-walled Spirit

I'm an un-walled spirit
Gazing past dark clouds
Bearing sorrow and pain;

A cardinal luring bloodworms
To surface with song bait,
Patience and stillness;

A child ignoring
An approaching storm,
Lingering in merriment;

A solitary left discovered,
Alone in a crowd be loved,
Enraptured ease.

Silent calm in rhythm
With harmony,
Knowing all peace,

I shout wordlessly
More silent than a whisper.
Do you hear me?

Respond then heart to heart
Touch to touch,
Eye to everlasting soul.

Terry Douglas

Finger-Touch

There's a finger-touch
Separating me from you,
A distance chasm-wide

In this reality
That closes when
I remain present—still.

Not sure you sense
Me stretching wide
Across this divide;

But I do love you,
And in that declaration
Two fingers touch.

Homecoming

They sleep together,
The young lovers,
The strong young bow,
The fitted curve,
Young bodies furled like wings,
Cupped like the land around the bay.
Here, the still deep water.
Found, found at least, the Other.
All the long searching over,
The imperative voices stilled.
Home, home at last, the safe harbor.
That emptiness at the primal core filled.
So, heart to heart,
In the shelter of his warmth,
I too slept in the arms of my Other,
Breathed in this soft concert,
Sweet, safe stillness of the soul,
I remember it.
If I woke them,
If I told them love cannot save them,
Love does not triumph,
They would not believe me.
Auschwitz, the strange car in the drive,
The classroom door, the doctor's face,
The sudden shadow of the plane,
All out there in the dark;
It cannot be.

I close the door.
They sleep, rocked on this warm tide,
For this brief time.
Immortal.

Bea DuRette

is a retired college professor of art history. Born in Georgia, she came as a military bride to Virginia in 1958, and lives in the same house today. A painter (three one-woman shows), folksinger, theater performer, gardener, cook, and hostess, she began an academic career at thirty-six, completing three degrees in five years. Her poetry was first published in *The Poet's Domain*, 2008; will also appear in *Skipping Stones*, 2009, forthcoming. She received a First Honorable Mention in the Poetry Society of Virginia's 2009 competition.

Bea DuRette

Spring Freeze

The daffodils were blooming
when the snow came down,
Five kinds, all over-weighted,
bent submitting low,
And then were buried whitely
in an unmarked mound;
So rare in coastal tidelands
where the Back Bay's blow
Of moisture usually turns the flakes
to wet grey rain.
In two days, frozen stiff, the unthawed
blooms emerged.
I broke them brittle; curious,
carried some inside
And put them with their sisters plucked
before the storm,
Sure that they'd thaw and dangle,
dead and wilted brides;
And was amazed when next I could not
tell the norm,
One from the other. Think, had I been
nine years frozen,
Thawing, little sisters, can they tell
How ice can run within the veins
yet still careen
Up to the blossoms as if all were well?
For one and forty years I turned to you
As if you were a mirror where I saw myself.
I can within my years the salvaged
daffodils arrange;
The resurrected white and yellow blooms
look out:
Do they perceive? How can they tell
what changed?

Bea DuRette

Parthenogen

Some of us find our path away.
Freedom lies horizons far
Where we're not known
As here we are.
We are not there our past, our names,
We are not even us.
There all is new.
My son and I, two of a mind,
With only our own selves at trust,
We found ourselves
Beyond the bounds
Of those who kept us as they knew;
A yearly glimpse, a brief quick call
Is all we need to reassure
Ourselves that nothing's changed at all;
What we left home in amber fixed.
Yet when we come to home again
And settle in familiar tides,
How strange to find the river's bend,
Old landmarks gone on certain sides
And in the graves
Names turned to bone.
Under our feet, new currents run.
Did we leave them the rivers by
Or was it our old world that spun?
Are they more blessed who seek no trace,
Who have no deep returning place,
Who find each strange day full of grace?
Now in my shadows come at last
Wherever he is now, is home,
Where he has chosen to belong:
He is his present, we the past.
His is the echo of my song.

Choose Something Like a Star

Bea DuRette

The Last Room

Here I am, Love, left behind
In this old house you loved and had so briefly.
You are close enough to touch today,
Alone in this old house with paint and plaster;
This is the last room, cleared away.
Square feet with me is still disaster,
And not a chance I've figured right.
If you were here, math would not matter;
You would look up, your eyes alight,
And grin at me, perched on this ladder.
You would be seventy and nine.
I can't imagine your quick body
Even so frail as it became
Before the end when death was kind:
A sleep within a sleep and no awaking.
Or did you, as I long to think, arise,
Delighted and surprised, as light was breaking
And come to kiss me, sleeping, one last time?
That would be sweetness undiminished;
But I have walls to caulk and prime
And this last room in your last dream
To finish.

The Poet's Domain

Bea DuRette

Annunciation

Anhinga
High up in the live-oak tree
Slowly stretching wings out to sun and light
Like a strange and
Terrifying angel
If he extended his snaky neck
And said to the barefoot girl
In the yard before
The unpainted cabin
Child
I have news for you
Must have been
Like that.

Choose Something Like a Star

Quite Nicely

Oh Star! That burns above my head—
The things to *only you* I've said
Of what my life has come to be.
You may not *listen*, but you *see*.

As I plow forward through my days
You watch me in your solemn way.
Yet not a censure, not a sound
Comes from your sphere so bright and round.

Do you approve? I dare not hope
To shine beneath *your* telescope,
But still you wait and watch with care,
A sentinel up in the air.

Sometimes I look with brimming soul
When weary days have claimed their toll
And find a solace in your face,
A quirky and irreverent grace.

While you don't speak, the heavens shout
And, saying naught, have found me out—
A speck upon a ball of clay
Over whom your ambit strays.

The earth revolves, the planets move—
Yet what does this momentum prove?
Your path above the earth is laid
And to the course you're ever staid.

Is there a message there for me?
Some secret that you'd have me see?
Perhaps it's just to lift my gaze
Beyond the sights of earthly days.

Are you not rooted where I see?
As much a slave to fate as me?
And yet, you soar—*so I will, too.*
Yes, something like a star will do.

Catherine Edwards

is a Southern poet with one husband, two children, and three cats. She is an unrepentant rhymer who fell in love with words at an early age and expects the honeymoon to go on forever.

The Poet's Domain

Nebula (as seen through telescope)

Lily of space,
beyond my sight,
beyond my dreams imagining,
why is your power, your beauty
so obscured?
Who sees you in that
dark and violent place . . .
or can I ask,
or should I ask
why you are there?

Margaret Edwards

(b. N.Y.C., 1932) has been writing for fun ever since she could hold a pencil. She has been published in chapbooks as well as in *The Poet's Domain*.

Remorse

I have dug
too shallow a grave
to bury my memories.
Flowers, planted above,
once glowing in the sun,
are overcome
by clouds of regret
rising from their bed
of restless repose.

Resting the memories
would destroy the flowers . . .
and so my life goes on
tinted by unforgiven hours.

Choose Something Like a Star

Nomads

Before millennia, we were travelers
following the seasons and the herds.
Our getting on was always hard-scrabble;
In sickness and in health, we had to move or die.
One day someone, somewhere, some way,
Learned to tame the food
We'd always wandered after. Then,
We started building fences;
Huts and walls began displacing tents;
And we became enclaves and called
Ourselves civilized. Back then,
We had to shout across the wind
On horseback to survive; at night
We talked in quiet tones and sometimes
Smoked or chewed. Always, we ate.
We burned our dead, let ash
And ember rise, returning to the stars.
Now, our conversations are but motes
Settled on convenience anywhere.
We shout at one another now so we
Don't have to hear; no one listens;
No one cares. No range remains
For flocks to crop, sparse game to hunt
On mountain sides. Polluted streams
Where we have long forgotten
Whence we came, and how and why.
The fences must come down,
The huts and monuments and walls.
We don't need place or property.
We must have space and movement,
Community of family and clan on horseback

Pete Freas

was born in Cleveland, Ohio and is a retired Navy helicopter pilot (twenty-six years), Vietnam vet, and retired Virginia teacher. Poet since childhood, Pete has published three chapbooks; founded Chesapeake Bay Poets where he maintains a website (chesbaypoets.org), edits *A Line In Time* (a weekly online newsletter of poetry events), and publishes *Skipping Stones* (an annual anthology of Hampton Roads poets and artists). He is currently working on two collections of poetry and two novels.

The Poet's Domain

Pete Freas

Following the seasons and the herds,
Scratching out survival. But where's
The open range? Where are the clans
That once we were? Now we ignore
The stars, pursue accumulated wealth,
And die in sterile rooms. We bury us,
Like farmers, in the soil. We've lost
Our presence, lost our way, and lost
Our bond with Earth and Moon and Sun.
We've lost our soul and time. We live
In noise and cannot take the world back.
We have forgotten life.

Choose Something Like a Star

Cat on Duke of Gloucester

I slept, woke, ate and went for a walk.
No one asked, few took notice. A drink from
the water fountain; a toll of one from the bell.
A gray and white cat sat on the cobblestones.
I crouched to pet her;
she pushed her head into my palm.

She saved my day.

Waiting
The Sound of Aging

The wind in my gaze
The pain running as the eve's dripping
The hours—they alone know my ways
The clock on the side table ticking

This I say to you—

A kiss of light on the head
A simple slow dance with oneself
A reason to find he said
A moment then is our wealth

Where are you?

Wheston Chancellor Grove

(b. October 1984) was born in northern California. He spent his early years on Magnolia Avenue in an 1880s Victorian, where he feels a certain anachronistic quality was imparted to him. He moved to Williamsburg, Va. in 1998. Mr. Grove believes you are as old as you feel and, inversely, finds he is obsolete in a generation that now communicates through a form of "verbal shorthand" i.e. IMs and texting. He has his own photography business, *Evergreen Stills*. He composes and frames pictures to preserve Time.

The one person in history with whom he would most like to speak, were she alive, is Sophie Scholl, co-author and peaceable activist for the White Rose resistance movement in Nazi Germany.

The Poet's Domain

Wheston Chancellor Grove

On Being Sophie Scholl

Will it hit me as an epiphany?
There's a tiger on this desk
and I'm thinking of those last minutes,
those last seconds before the razor of absolute
silenced her body but not her voice.
Execution passed, black hats and a sinister
curtain revealed the stark cutting board.
"The heaviest hour" it was said
when the mind knows
not where it is going. Can the spirit by its own
hold consciousness apart from the tangible self?
How terrifying to see oneself severed. The instant
of blow, pray be swift. And the release,
no soul returns
as its prior form, to speak of.
How then do we look death in the face and
then back at each other,
with the knowledge
we are going, we are going, we are going.
To love, to protect, until the hour of loss . . .
Courage yes.

Choose Something Like a Star

Water

I should spend more time watching water
Something like a creek, a river, an ocean
Some liquid that moves
Reflects the light
Something that hides and yet reveals

I should look at waves that flatten
And grow thin as they climb the beach
Then trickle back beneath themselves

I should look at waterfalls that seem
to let go, pitching forward
An endless pouring of white
Like a falling star

Or rapids that whirl their way between rocks
Racing, pushing everything before them

I should cast my lure into a lake
Believing a fish will strike my bait

I should dive into a deep, deep pool
Knowing I can swim down as far as it goes

I should look
and learn
and never forget what is there
What is real.

Doris Gwaltney

is the author of two adult novels, *Shakespeare's Sister*, and *Duncan Browdie, Gent*. Her middle grade novel, *Homefront*, was published by Simon & Schuster Books for Young Readers. Her collection of performance monologues, *A Mirror in Time, History in First Person*, was published by ScriptWorks Press in 2007. She teaches for LifeLong Learning at Christopher Newport University, and lives in Smithfield, Va.

The Poet's Domain

Once and Future Buddies

Joe and I met
September 1936
Second grade
Playing and joking
Joe made school
Less frightening
We became best friends

An excellent student
Joe took school easy
Perhaps it was all
A game to him
Finishing high school
At the top of our class
Joe skipped college
Went to work
Married young
Stayed local

I went away
To college, the army
Sent me to Germany
Discharged in Europe
I studied in Paris
Back in the U.S.A.
I worked in California,
Manhattan, and New Jersey
Thirty years gone
I came back home
Joe and I worked together
Much seemed unchanged

William L. Hickey

born in 1929, is a square dancer and retired information analyst. His interest in poetry began with the study of the fifteenth century French poet, François Villon.

Choose Something Like a Star

William L. Hickey

Some years later
At a friend's funeral
Joe's wife took me aside
Dementia, she said
I held on to the pew
Knees failing
Even church pews
Now seem unsteady
One thing left
To hold tight to
The deep-rooted memories
Of well-aged friendship.

Flat Calm

Half asleep, fighting sleep, sails hanging lifeless above at midnight,
Beyond the mast, the deep of night salutes our fate,

I search for breeze, any breeze, the promise of which would still the rigging,
Stop the slap of sheets, ease the oppressive heat of July,

Silence the clap of halyards and yield a steered course,
My touch on the tiller is without result, as millions of stars can witness,

Hundreds of miles of dark Atlantic, flat and glassy as far as we can see
From this rocking cradle we see the stars in countless numbers,

And we are carried east to Bermuda by a silent river beneath the stillness,
Without a breeze for us to break the grip below,

I need only one star, yet I see millions,
There is only now to wait for morning and the wind with it.

3:00 A.M. the anchor on deck grins, tempting me,
I could let it drop overboard for a mile and it would strike nothing,

---

Steven S. Hollberg is a certified public accountant and resides in Urbanna, Virginia with his wife, Wanda, a stained glass and fused glass artist, and son Ellery. He is a graduate of the College of William and Mary and Virginia Commonwealth University. He has served on the town council of Urbanna, Middle Peninsula Planning District Commission, Chesapeake Bay Public Access Authority, and Middle Peninsula Business Development Partnership. He grew up on the Chesapeake Bay, sailing competitively there and offshore.

Steven S. Hollberg

A freighter crosses our bow, reducing its speed, a low and lumbering growl,
It missed us by a thousand yards, but would the next?

The stars above me wink at the prank, the silent sea stretches in repose,
The crew snores heavily, I return to fighting sleep.

Morning seems a thousand hours away
While we are adrift.

Night Sail

The salt stings
A sky full of stars above and a bay full of waves beneath,
We lift up slowly and then fall into the next trough,

The wind whistles in the jib track, rising in pitch,
Then recedes as a whisper into the night air, a mournful suggestion of an aria, a lone voice

Neither gleeful nor mournful, without emotion, like the beacon to starboard
A mechanical winking, regardless how the seas tear at it,

The voice of the track is a passionless whistle rising and falling, cutting the air,
A strange lullaby that haunts me from years past when I recall the liberty of my youth,

The Poet's Domain

Steven S. Hollberg

Spent chasing imaginary pirates down the Chesapeake Bay,
Legs dangling overboard and trails of phosphorous blobbing up from below the hull,

I know the compass course, I feel the wind and I gauge the speed,
I pick a star that favors all three and burst through the night,

Rounding the Vineyard, besting the tidal change,
The salt stings my eyes, but the pain is joy,

I aim for Regulus, and hear Leo's roar in the seas rush
And my youth carried away in the night's wake.

Star

Star is a verb. Star is a noun.
Star is a babe in a beautiful gown.
Star is a twinkle high in the sky.
Star is a signal after, "Goodbye."

Peggy Kelly

was born in Washington, D. C., and graduated from the University of Maryland. She and Bob have four boys and four grandchildren. Peggy and Bob live in Newport News, Virginia, just off the James River.

The Poet's Domain

Compass

Though he grew up in the tiniest town
on a Montana mountainside,
he came alive to music of Gounod,
quoted Shakespeare to the sunrise,
and English poets to us kids; all
points of his compass built in
four years' study of fine arts.
Dad amazed my sisters and me until
we found compasses of our own.

Robert L. Kelly

grew up in Tacoma, Washington, became a naval architect and marine engineer. He met and married his wife, Peggy, in Washington, D. C. They have four sons and four grandchildren. In 1990, Bob retired from Newport News Shipbuilding Company in Newport News. He now enjoys poetry classes with Patricia Flower Vermillion at Christopher Newport University.

Stabilization

In the great quietude of the nave
I pause before the altar in solitude
remembering the rush of His love
flooding, filling this sanctuary
yesterday and feel it still this
Monday morning as I drop my
jar of peanut butter in the basket for
lunches at St. Paul's, then go to the
volunteer desk for my weekly turn
answering the phone stabilized
by my greatest love.

Robert L. Kelly

Hotel Soap

O soap (The only bar in sight),
I grant your mysterious fragrance the right
To some obscurity in wrapper—
It will not do to say of water
Since water is what brings out your delight.
Some mystery becomes your paper shroud.
But to be wholly scentless
In your wrapper is not allowed.

Release your effusion of delight.
Make me rejoice this dismal night.
Release your bouquet, a whiff says it's floral.
But of what flowers, what intensity?
Release peony, release rose,
Providing scents to fill my nose.
Captivate me with your floral blend.

Dry, you give me nothing for my
Weary, poor, paupered psyche.
Alone in a city strange and cold,
Wife not here, feeling old.
Naked in steaming shower I rip
off your flimsy paper wrapper.

Ecstatic essences don't fill the night.
Your scent, suggesting a rose, is very slight.
Slighter still as I slather your lather giving
Only a hint in this shower of a garden bower.
Just my luck. No perfumed delight
To ease this tedium this dreary night.

The Poet's Domain

Robert L. Kelly

Their Lodestar

Each morning out they go, rain or snow,
by car, by bus, bicycle, on the run
like other shipbuilders today and of long ago.

Constructing aircraft carriers well they know;
steel ships, tough ships, biggest under the sun;
each morning out they go in rain or snow.

Carriers designed to sting the foe
when roused to anger the fiercest ship bar none.
Like other shipbuilders today and of long ago

They build submarines that cruise below
giving enemy ships a deadly lesson.
Each morning out they go, rain or snow

"Building Good Ships," the lodestar they follow,
always before them, shining in every season.
Like other shipbuilders today and of long ago

Happy, or mad, or sick, well they know
following their lodestar must be done.
Each morning our they go in rain or snow
like other shipbuilders today and of long ago.

Choose Something Like a Star

In Loving Memory of

What we come down to
is a small card printed in the U.S.A.,
a verse handed out to mourners
on why no one should grieve.
It is what we leave behind.
It is our last thing.
We are curled in church pews,
tucked in old black purses,
dropped at gravesides.
Only a few will carry home
the record of our birth,
the day we "went to God."
But who knows where we go.
For some small time we lay
in desk drawer corners,
in pockets of a pin-striped funeral suit.
We might become a bookmark,
may earn a brief notation
in the journal of a friend.
How much better would it be
if someone bought for us an unnamed star,
keeping the receipt that shows
exactly where we are.
Otherwise, forgotten programs
with our "name inserted here"
will be all that escapes the grave.

Maddie Kline

is a freelance writer residing in Delaware. Her poetry has appeared in volumes 23 and 24 of *The Poet's Domain*, and volume seven of *In Good Company*.

Maddie Kline

Stardust

I do not like the stars.
They say too much
of just how small we are.
Beneath their bed of blackness
lie the ashes of our prayers,
light-blinded, burned away.
Bright barriers between our God
and theirs, no answer comes
unless that winking laughter might be one.
Perhaps the stars exist to show
the end of our beginning,
to prove that we have always been alone.

Heavensense

I fell into the night sky
when I was six years old.
A friend and I were resting
in a farmer's barley field,
forgetting to clutch the earth
to keep from tumbling in.
We had been warned
that vertigo would come,
and in its spinning, pull us upward,
turn us into something like a star.
If we had not let go,
we could have watched
through keyholes in God's heaven,
how He greets those souls
who cannot hold their ground.

Choose Something Like a Star

a hard one to read

Like a bruise, my words surface
with their own color,
form a painful patch above my heart,
a flag that signals where love starts
and stops, where it begins
and ends and what comes of words
that try to tell
what it means
and that love seems
to have been
a poem stuck
deep within
me.

Barry M. Koplen

In 1968, one of Barry's earliest poems won a prize. Since then, his poetry has appeared in collegiate magazines, many Net sites, and in newspapers. In 2004, his poem, "Joseph", was published in *Breath of Parted Lips*, a hardback collection published by the Robert Frost Place. In 2007, two of Barry's poems were included in the collection of the 100 best poems submitted from the last five years to a Chesapeake Bay area literary review. Currently, Barry serves as a lecturer at Danville Community College and attends Queens University's MFA program.

dog-eared time

Before I knew your birthday,
each day was like the one before.
Yet now you have joined that relatives calendar
of gifts or cards or weighty tributes
on certain boldly numbered days
I dread forgetting. Before then,
you were first lilacs in spring
or bright green to me as Irish clover;
you were a constellation I yearned to see
return, a burning red oak
whose leaves married a winter rain;
you were Israel, its shofar sound,
unique as an old world bleating at the new.
Now you are a day, a date that does not look
at all like you.
Forgive me
for not crossing off that daunting reminder
until my fresh Kona warms
like yours when your coffeed lips
were sometimes mine.

Barry M. Koplen

and you ask why

It was that last kiss, your last kiss,
how it interrupted our goodbye the way
a sonnet reshapes a crescent moon,
restores its shadowed parts,
re-filters its light the way your mouth
covered my words,
canceled our parting,
framed me as a back-lit constellation.

catfish

Double anchors drop, hold,
moor us at fifty feet
where the ledge plateaus
then falls a hundred more.

As promised, I'd beaten the sunset.
My date asks what I do out here,
when I tire of worms and lures,
reels and poles, as I pile cushions
on the deck.

There, after stars come,
I shine my crappie light,
my magnet to seine short-lived shad.
We rock in a quiet breeze.

I fetch my guitar,
cast my cradling songs past her,
into darkness where prayers go,
into its catfish essence.

As she sleeps,
I'm set to feel my hook touch bottom.

Choose Something Like a Star

After Winter Solstice

"In the bleak midwinter"
the rhythm of the seasons
beats beneath the snow and ice.
Days lengthen
as earth spins
on its path
around the sun.
Facing the western sky
I mark the sunsets
on the windowsill
with my pencil,
proving to my doubting self
that the world goes on,
implacably
but also unerringly,
and if it does
then so must we.

A Poet Reads from His Work

Twice the words are spoken, twice heard—
a surface skimming, then deeper,
plunging into the bloody depths
of his journey through a dark wood.
His candle glow lights the way
for our own Pilgrim's Progress.
A trail blazer—he cuts a blaze
on each tree along the path
for those who dare to follow.

Margaret P. Latham (b. 1920, Lexington, Mo.) graduated from the College of William and Mary; earned her master of nursing degree at what is now Case/Western Reserve. She has made five collections of her poetry. This is her seventh appearance in *The Poet's Domain*. She lives in Charlottesville, Va.

The Poet's Domain

Margaret P. Latham

The Summer Person

One arrives at the summer cottage,
a refugee fleeing
the cacophonous honking of taxi horns,
the sucking swish of subway trains.
Here, the early morning sound
is of a mockingbird perched in a blue lace
hydrangea
spreading its Van Gogh blossoms
next to the glowing daylilies.

The silence is daunting.
Why have I isolated myself from my
accustomed life,
thinking to get away from it all?
The unmatched dishes and old pots,
the musty salt marsh smell,
the spider webs and mosquitoes, all . . .
all are unsettling.
Perhaps I can purchase a city paper,
read it from front to back,
or see if the ancient television works.

However . . .
as days go by, I find myself settling down
to the rhythm of the tides,
the rising and setting of the sun,
the phases of the moon.
Egret, osprey, cormorant, and gull,
my daily companions.
Finally, one day as the sun sets across the bay,
I realize . . .

This is my peaceable kingdom.
This is my summer home.

Choose Something Like a Star

Give Us This Day . . .
(Re "Staff of Life" Superstar, (*)
Michael Charles Antil, Sr.)
(10/02/1902–03/04/1973)

Dad would be up and gone
before we all awoke—
to solve phoned crises nightly
interrupting sleep,
and checking bread trucks loading
(pre-dawn schedules to keep—
bringing the staff of life
of which the poets spoke.)

As teen bakeshop worker,
Dad said he "got the call"
after tumbling down an elevator shaft—
believing God's message was
that he choose this craft—
since bread cartons on ground floor
had cushioned his fall.

Fresh, daily, baked goods
to replenish empty shelves
in hospitals, jails,
restaurants, and groceries
came from the smooth,
coordinated energies
of a hard-working,
early-morning crew of elves . . .

Dad often let us visit
this enchanted place . . .
where whirling vats held
shiny, swirling, twisting globs
these white-clad figures pummeled,
shaped into white blobs. . .
then, let rise, expand,
until filling twice the space . . .

Mary Antil Lederman

(b. 1925, Los Angeles, Calif.) AB, magna cum laude, Syracuse University, 1946; M. Ed., University of Virginia, 1968, retired in 1987 after twenty-three years as foreign language teacher/chair at Albemarle High School in Charlottesville, Virginia. (For the past several years she has enjoyed sharing selections from salvaged, French textbooks with fellow Francophone members of "Le Cercle Français" at the Senior Center in Charlottesville, Virginia.) Her poems have appeared in twenty-four volumes of *The Poet's Domain*, and in numerous other publications, including the 1993 and 2003 anthologies of the Poetry Society of Virginia.

(*)www.breadforschoolsrun.org

The Poet's Domain

Mary Antil Lederman

Tin carpets on which
this magic soaring happened
were swiftly slid onto hot,
waiting oven racks . . .
then, gilded mounds rode
regally down rolling tracks
to benign guillotines
awaiting at the end . . .

Huge barrels underneath
would catch each falling crumb—
to be collected, bagged,
and sold for livestock feed—
each morsel of this product
nourishing a need.
(I still can smell the bread—
and hear the knife blades hum . . .)

No perfume wafting
from the finest burned incense
could tantalize the senses
more than that released
from pliant, kneaded dough,
impregnated with yeast—
leaving birth ovens, golden brown,
in full fragrance . . .

"The baking industry,"
Dad often proudly said,
"is the only trade the Lord
mentioned in His Prayer."
Leavened with a God-given
energy and flair,
Dad's *holy orders* were
to provide *daily bread*.

Choose Something Like a Star

Mary Antil Lederman

Supernovas . . . Gone Too Soon(*)

We must say far too many good-byes,
And we must sigh far too many sighs
For too many grim, unanswered "Whys"—
Such as, "Who lives today?" and "Who dies?"

Our hearts hum in chorus life's sad song
That our tears help compose all life long . . .

We suffer far too many regrets
Of past failings one never forgets—
All the unpaid, emotional debts—
And pain that indifference begets.

Our hearts hum in chorus life's sad song
That our tears help compose all life long. . .

It's the surcharge we must pay for life—
With all happiness tempered by strife—
And laughter and sobs equally rife
Between lovers and friends, man and wife.

Our hearts hum in chorus life's sad song
That our tears help compose all life long . . .

We're all like gay minstrels in mourning—
Masks changing with little forewarning—
With comedy's from eve to morning
Into tragedy's mask transforming.

Our hearts hum in chorus life's sad song
That our tears help compose all life long . . .

(*) Michael C. Antil, Sr., October 2, 1902–March 4, 1973
Michael C. Antil, Jr., November 15, 1932–March 26, 1988
Richard F. Antil, December 15, 1935–December 31, 1993
Aidan Graham Lederman, July 7, 1977–June 13, 1994
Mary Holman R. Antil, October 29, 1903–March 5, 1996
Dorothy Antil Bredesen, July 20, 1929–January 3, 2007
Paul Robert Antil, January 14, 1939 –August 5, 2007

Mary Antil Lederman

Not "In the Stars"

On astral signs the seers rely
For portents as to when persons die.

Their horoscopes, "written in the sky,"
May explain "when"—but never "why?"

Étoile du Ballet? (Jamais!) ("Fat Chance!")

Chagrined by recent new girth gain—
and tutu strain—
that inflates seams
and deflates dreams
of fame in le ballet de corps—
our Terpsichore
tries to disguise
her ample thighs,
before tryout, with lacy frill—
that she hopes will
make tutu be
ampler "three-three"!

Choose Something Like a Star

Mary Antil Lederman

Tercet
*Tribute to a stellar educator,
John Ashley Blackburn, professor emeritus,
University of Virginia

Watching the ground while stepping carefully
to avoid foot hazards one might not see,
(that can trip up ambulant elderly . . .)

in somber thought . . . in sad, dark mood
subdued . . .
(despite bright sunlight in the neighborhood,
where the church of our friend's funeral stood)

when I glimpsed it—shiny, beckoning, round—
a Lincoln penny, face up, on the ground . . .
Then, feet apart, a second, third I found!

"Pennies from Heaven? —in a straight line
(as, wryly, perhaps, a "Heaven-cent sign"
from "The Great Emancipator" divine—

in praise of His earthly ambassador,
educational emancipator,
for student equal civil rights labor?)

John A. Blackburn, Jefferson's legatee,
helped bring academic diversity
to its founder's famed university—

and left it, educators, friends agree,
"as Jefferson intended it to be"—
and as John Blackburn's stellar legacy.

(*) tercet: a group of three lines rhyming together (terza rima)

Morning Stars

Staggering outside at five in the morning
I'm under a sky filled with stars.

I walk over the deserted parking lot
and look at dead leaves in my path.

Another morning paper next to the laundromat
lit in neon to make it seem bleaker.

In the morning sky I see the Little Dipper
and single stars in infinite spaces.

The paper is about wars and disasters
but it's part of the day like a cup of tea.

The stars seem more comforting in their places.
We come and go but they keep on shining.

Joseph Lewis

(b. Pittsburgh, Pa.) has published poems in several previous volumes of *The Poet's Domain*. He lives in Williamsburg, Va.

Joseph Lewis

Listening to Bach

I can forget myself as Bach plays
on my little metal box of music,

and sunlight spreads on the grass
not withered like it was in winter

when I seemed to die a thousand deaths.
Now the trees repeat the old story

that's existed before we ever appeared,
the seasons changing as the earth turns

on an axis Newton wrote only God created
instead of from the complicated equations

he devised to explain how stars move
the same way the Brandenburg Concertos

seem to move with the same precision
here on a sunny day centuries later

as I hear them trying to forget myself
for the time the music is playing.

Prelude

the sky
flickering
like a malfunctioning light bulb:
a far away lightning
dressed with the sound of distant thunder . . .
the humid wind
threatening
pushing
away the late afternoon
into a premature darkness:
the color of tumult

to the clapping of nervous hands
cats are called in
dogs scramble to their masters
doors are slammed shut
against the tempestuousness of trees:
their violent sound
their shaking branches
chasing everyone into shelter:
a tangible reminder of the constant
that rules all things
that is in all things
that is not a constant
that is the cause and effect
in a universe
of change

D. S. Lliteras

is the author of ten books, which have received national and international acclaim. In the last twenty years, his poetry and short stories have appeared in numerous periodicals and anthologies. His most recent novel, *The Master of Secrets*, was published in March 2007.

D. S. Lliteras

Mortal

Autumn:
not a time for dying
but Fall
just a time for changing:
The weather,
a bit cooler
The flora,
not quite as full
The sun,
with its different heat
    more seen
    than summer felt
The sky, bluer through the trees
    and not
    because of color.
All this changing,
and yet
    all is the same,
Mortal
    is the cycle.

The Poet's Domain

April One

Of all the twelve, my fav'rite month
occurs in early Spring.
The gentle rain, the sunny days,
well, nearly everything.

However, what enthralls me most
is poetry I write.
Of course I'm good throughout the year,
but April I ignite

a fire in those most blest to hear
my scintillating rhyme.
I owe my many fans more now
than any other time.

I've had this talent ever since
I showed it off in school.
And if you drink this potion down—
you are my April Fool!

The Limericker

A poem-a-day is my goal;
they say that it's good for my soul.
I doubt that they mean
a limerick obscene
so I'll keep this one under control.

There once was a poet from Troy;
his rhyme and his meter brought joy
to fam'ly and friends
but there it all ends,
for everyone else they'd annoy.

Edward W. Lull

began writing poetry at age 65 after two earlier careers: one as a Navy submarine officer; then as a business executive. He has published three books of his poetry: *Cabin Boy to Captain; a Sea Story; Where Giants Walked;* and *The Sailors: Birth of a Navy*; edited a poetry anthology; and co-edited a poetry teaching guide. He runs monthly poetry readings in the Williamsburg Regional Library at Norge, and, for the past ten years, a three-day poetry festival every May. He teaches beginning and intermediate poetry writing workshops for the Christopher Wren Association at the College of William and Mary. He and his wife, Evelyn, live in Williamsburg.

Edward W. Lull

For Sale by Bob

Among the things I like the least
the one I place right at the top
is looking for a four-wheel beast
and dealing with a used-car shop.

The salesmen there use many means
including mystic hocus-pocus.
About the cars they don't know beans;
can't tell a Mustang from a Focus.

If I preferred the Chevy line,
a Monte Carlo I might get,
or Malibu would do just fine;
but Bob showed me a red Corvette.

Toyota cars are good on gas:
both Camry and Corolla too.
But salesman Bob showed all his class,
suggesting a Dodge Dart in blue.

Are used-car salesmen all the same?
They seem to be a lot like Bob.
My needs or wants are not their aim,
it's make the sale or lose their job.

The Poet's Domain

Underwater Ballet

The sea cocoon
born of raindrops,
of rushing rivers,
caresses the land.
God's other world.

Not always
in harmony within its silent depths
but beautiful in
its secret dissonance.

A world of rainbow-dipped
creatures
performing an
underwater ballet
in ever-moving liquid motion.
A jeté
pas de bourrée
pas de deux
God's
underwater ballet

Known
but to those who
break through
earth's watery cocoon
to reach its noiseless depths.

Betty Maistelman

graduated with honor from Ohio University, Athens, Ohio, with a degree in journalism. Her feature stories have been published in magazines and newspapers. American Greetings Corporation purchased four of Betty's humorous studio booklets. Harcourt Educational Measurement purchased her stories and poems for testing materials for children. Her poems were published in The Poetry Society of Virginia 80*th* Anniversary Anthology of Poems, *The Poet's Domain, Skipping Stones*, and a short story was published in *In Good Company*. She is currently writing children's picture books, middle-grade novels, and poetry.

Choose Something Like a Star

Stars on Earth
Inspired by and dedicated to Dr. Daisy Murphy,
beloved friend and colleague

The lightness of spring continues to overtake
the darkness of winter as the once gloomy
and sometimes angry clouds
make way for the rebirth of life and all its
wonders.
A time of rejuvenation, spring comforts us
with its warm sunbeams playing hide and seek
while enticing us to join in the fun.
The diamond-shaped patterns of a nearby lake
sparkle and wink as they reflect the sun's kisses.
The tender blade of a young shoot of grass
serenely flutters in the gentle caress of a sudden
breeze.
Bumble bees buzzz beguilingly in the hopes of
making merry with as many flowers-in-waiting
as possible.
Mother Nature would, no doubt, approve
of the lightness and brightness that spring
continually brings
because just as darkness is despair draped in
doom,
lightness offers the hope for a new beginning,
a new you.
Thus, people disguised as lightness become
our stars on Earth
shining here, there, everywhere
while beckoning us to do
that which we are called to do,

Mary L. Martin

an English adjunct at Tidewater Community College in Portsmouth, Va., has been writing poetry since she was sixteen years old. She is a published author and poet whose works have frequently appeared in *Skipping Stones*. She was recently nominated by her peers at TCC to receive the Faculty Showcase Award for 2008, which was the first time an adjunct ever received this award in the history of TCC. Mary is currently teaching in her fifth learning community for students in developmental writing classes. Her poem, "The Mighty, Mighty Dendrites," has been selected for publication in Dr. Rita Smilkstein's, a nationally and internationally reknowned researcher on how the brain learns; to be published later this year.

The Poet's Domain

Mary L. Martin

which is to become a beacon of brightness
for those who are struggling in a quagmire
of desperation
because of lost jobs, savings, and unpaid bills.
So, become a star on which others can hang
their hopes, wishes, and dreams.
Most importantly, because of who you are
and what you do,
make the once-thought impossible dreams of
others come true, too.

Synchronicity

Accidents that shouldn't happen
Coincidences that do
Natural events that devastate
Rebuilding communities that unite
Rebuking intolerance
Embracing diversity
Not speaking
Empathetic listening
Chaos all over the world
The glorious music of the spheres
Thinking without speaking
Finishing another's sentences
Compatibility and connection
With this world as we know it
Harmony and affinity for the world beyond
That which we can only imagine
A mutual regard for peaceful coexistence
That's long past due . . .
Harmonious, simultaneous connections
Synchronicity

In the Glass

The sound of the sun is muffled
by the killing dark.
Even in the dark, light lingers in the shadow
of stars.
In the maze we tread our history through
fallacy of true lies.

In the killing dark
we cannot find the way,
in the maze we tread our history through
fallacy of true lies.
Daily we cope with minutia.

We cannot find the way,
only cope hour to hour.
Daily we cope with minutia,
only to have seconds fall hourglass fine.

Coping hour to hour,
even in the dark, light lingers in the shadow
of stars.
Seconds fall hourglass fine.
The sound of the sun is muffled.

Megan K. McDonald

started writing in a junior high school creative writing class in Hawaii, but other than yearly Christmas poems did not continue her writing for twenty years. She credits her restart to poetry to an article in the *Washington Post* about a long-running Virginia poetry venue. After attending a meeting of Poet's Anonymous in 1995 she generated two poems and has been writing ever since. She has been published in *Poet's Anonymous* (Virginia) anthologies, *Poet's Anonymous* (United Kingdom) anthology, *Poetry Just for You, Event Horizon* and *The Poet's Domain*.

The Poet's Domain

Megan K. McDonald

Stepping Out of Shadows

Safe in the shadows,
lost in the refraction of dapples
I pause between light and dark
contemplating the next step.

Lost in the refraction of dapples
I weigh the past and the future.
I hold tight to youthful fancies
and long to step away.

I pause between light and dark
between safety and uncertainty
I look for your coming
and crouch again in shadow.

Contemplating the next step
I shatter the bonds of safety
cover my fear
and step into death and love.

Sunsets

in the desert the
fraction of light before
clear unseeing dark

in broad leaf forests
a dance of light breaks
dancing shadows

on the ocean a
path glows refraction of day
before stars drown

under snow fall
the sun melts into
the soft dream time

Megan K. McDonald

Can a Shadow Be a Friend?

Can a shadow be a
friend if it leaves
with the rising of the dark?
When stranded alone with
only surrounding darkness,
how can you reach out,
touch a shape you
cannot see? False
light shining day and
night hoping to pin love
to my side
but love like shadows
remains illusive, still
disappearing with the rising
of the dark. To those
who cannot share the
dark—you also do not
belong to the light.
So we all still travel
alone—searching for
those unafraid to step
alone, but then I
too am only a shadow.

Megan K. McDonald

Moon Bath

sky light gone
ugh—hunt again

i sun watch
sun sky gone
cower in darkness

i watch the skies
the sun father sky is eaten
restored. we praise the heavens.

i watch the moon bathe
the earth with shadow
mask the sun,
dance for a galactic second
crowning the sun with golden
glowing corona.

Choose Something Like a Star

Amy Vanderbilt

Here was a woman
who knew what to do
and told us the same
in 738 pages soft as sable.
Everywhere she went
she looked for the rise
of new forms and
the decline of old habits.

This is where she stood.
She traced the frame of
her second-story window—
smooth sill, upright jambs,
the head uncomplaining,
mullions and muntins
codifying the view.

It was the glass that troubled her.
No matter how framed in propriety,
the panes stood there,
squares of time turned to ice,
clear as the eyes of old wives,
demanding the homage of velvet
and sheers to mask the presence
of their unrestrained vision.

She knew it would be the opposite
of good taste to board them over
or even to paint them out.
So, every morning and afternoon
she must walk by the window
shackled by corners, shaded
with silk, yet admitting
relentless light and disorder.

It was here
she shattered transparent sand
and found opaque earth.

Anne Meek

is a retired educator originally from Tennessee who moved to Alexandria, Virginia, in 1987 to serve as managing editor of *Educational Leadership* at the Association for Supervision and Curriculum Development. Anne serves as an associate editor for *Skipping Stones*, the regional poetry and art anthology edited and published by Pete Freas at Mindworm Press in Chesapeake, Virginia. Anne has had twenty-five or thirty poems published in various journals, such as the *Tennessee Poetry Journal*; *The Small Farm*; *The Phoenix*; *Plainsong*; *Windless Orchard*, and others.

Anne Meek

Secret Funds

It's not time to go
But already
My substance
Is melting
And trickling down
The highway
West,
Sniffing
Like money
On the trail of a Swiss bank,
      A proper place
For quiet accumulation
While my resources ripen
Until the time is right.
      Then they'll find
My exoskeleton, an empty
Skin of Lycra Spandex,
Along with dust and doghair
Upon the kitchen floor.

Anne Meek

From Lisa's Porch
for Gil

A lazy sundown wind meanders
through the trees in the backyard,
rattling leaves and branches and
pushing puffs of gray and white
across a sky of constant blue.

Suddenly my cell phone vibrates,
and I'm startled. The wind's
in my pocket? No, it's someone
searching for me—it's you—
looking for connection, for love.

We talk about the day while
sun and clouds skip and shine,
now light, now shadow,
separating, then coming together
across the tree-framed sky.

Listen! Did you hear that whistle?
The evening Amtrak's arriving
in Winter Park—echoing
that lonesome wail of trains
we heard in childhood,

long before we met,
long before this eventide
of our lives. Now, at dusk,
I want you with me,
so far, yet so near,

until the sun is gone,
the wind is quiet,
the night takes over, and
the owl speaks again and again
from within the darkness.

The Poet's Domain

Anne Meek

Shy

There I was
>   wondering when
>   to let you in on
>   my secret,
>   saving it
>   because
>   I didn't know you well
>   and I wanted to be sure
>   you would not be
>   unreceptive—well, harsh—
>   about my poems
>   and
>   because
>   I like secrets.

Then suddenly
there you were
>   standing before me
>   brown-eyed
>   brown-sweatered
>   and somewhat shy—
>   because
>   you did not know me well
>   and you wanted to be sure
>   I would not be harsh?—
>   handing me a literary collage
>   showing me the pages
>   where your poems were—
>   letting me in on your secret
>   and walking swiftly away,
>   leaving me poetry in print
>   and also
>   poetry in mind.

Anne Meek

The Genealogy of Raisin-Filled Cookies

I.
Descended from Banbury tarts—
The kind you eat—earliest notice
We have found is "... *flat pastries
With spicy, currant fillings*"...
"1586 or earlier.". . . Came over
From England after that,
Not sure which ship, but
Are searching passenger lists.

Could have been in pocket
Of someone from Banbury Cross.
Made their way in memory
Southward through the colonies,
Looking for land resembling home—
Oxfordshire it was, bit north
And west of London.

II.
Not sure how they came to
Kentucky, but about 1930
The record is clear: Mother's
Recipes include "Raisin-Filled Cookies
From Mrs. Harry Whitehead"—
> Mother of Don Whitehead,
> Who helped clear the
> Field of rocks, when Dad
> Was Harlan's first football coach.

But I digress.
We are tracing the ancestry of
These sugar-encrusted cookies,
Still known in the old country
As Banbury cakes, still famous
Where that fine lady rode

The Poet's Domain

Anne Meek

That white horse, and still created
From secret recipes, like bourbon.

III.
Over the years the gene pool
Changed, of course—puff paste
Was not to be found in Early
Kentucky, nor currants,
Nor much in the way of spices—
Just wild grapes, and by the
1920s, raisins from Fresno.

So in their various kitchens,
The mothers of the clan
Gave birth to new generations
Of the well-remembered and
Much-loved ancestral cakes,
Spreading the line into
Tennessee, Massachusetts,
Virginia, Heaven knows where—

IV.
That is why today
I can share with you
The umpteenth generation
Of Banbury tarts, these
Raisin-filled cookies
From Kentucky.

Did you taste the lemon zest
In the teacake crust of these
21st century cousins—
How it contrasts the vanilla, yet
Echoes the currants and spice?

Piano Fingers

My sister claps her hands
on the kitchen table.
My slapstick joke.
Her delicate, tapered hands.
Her fingers are happy.
They are laughing.
Long fingers. Piano fingers,
Mom said years ago
from her Irish side.
She did not see the old Italian
women cross themselves
when they skimmed the surface
of her daughter's obtuse eyes.
Today the cat's head melts
in my sister's delicate hand
and my dog's face leaps
into her long piano fingers.
My fingers are happy.
They are laughing, too.
Short fingers. Italian work hands,
Mom said from my father's side.
Small fingers. Grateful fingers,
growing longer as they write poetry
below the surface of my sister's
loving eyes.

Elaine Morgan is a poet and freelance writer. Her works have most recently appeared in *Earth's Daughters, Out of Line, Sacred Journey, Candor, Common Ground Review, The Poet's Domain, ArtWord Quarterly,* among many others. She has received awards from *Byline Magazine* and the Poetry Society of Virginia. She is a three-time Senior Poet Laureate for the State of Virginia through the Kitchener Foundation.

The Poet's Domain

Elaine Morgan

Still Point

Guido Reni scrutinizes the model he has chosen to portray the Queen. She's plump. Beautiful. Her coloring satisfies. Hair. Eyes. Perfect size. Would she kill herself if she lost a war, or choose life as a trophy for a Caesar in a foreign land?

Great Horned Owl's feet are big.
Big as her hand.
Razor-sharp talons protrude. She contemplates the sixty-inch wing span, starched ear tufts, narrowing chrome yellow eyes. When he tilts backwards, will he slash?

Guido dives below the surface of the model, searching for her essence under the smiling tranquil mask. Is there sufficient pride? Would she ever clasp an asp?

Inching closer to the injured wild owl, empathy, fear, and raw passions collide. Chrome-yellow merges with unflinching dark brown eyes. Is the blank canvas on her side? Does she dare? Should she run and hide?

Guido spies a wistful tear about to say goodbye in Cleopatra's watery right eye. She pulls the snake to her breast and prepares to die.

Great Horned Owl splashes vivid colors of lost power, survival, and a longing for another starlit flight. Florescent lighting blinds. She heals in artificial light.

Elaine Morgan

Candles flicker. Light and shadows twine.
Pigment glides. Shades of life, death,
wounding, healing arise. Cleopatra hugs
the asp. Owl's broken wing is cast.
Guido sadly waves goodbye.
She heaves a quiet sigh.
Still point unifies.

Shaman on the Via Positiva

The forest in early morning. Trees barren of
leaves, anorexic against the canvas of a
slate gray sky. A mockingbird sips rain
drops from a dried oak leaf. Lone Hawk
tilts its head upwards, wings outstretched,
worshipping the retreating rays of the tepid
winter sun. Fourteen Canada geese herald
their journey to the icy water of the lake.
Two swoop and skim the forest floor, levitat-
ing in poetic choreography.

He walks in the shadows of sunlight.
Phantoms dance in darkness, resurrected
in the lukewarm splintered sun. He awakes
and dreams of dead crows shouting revelry.
Great Spirit calls his name saying, *Do not*
weep. You are not alone. Shake the rattle.
They may return.
Old Shaman giggles, knowing life is paradoxical. He chases all the ghosts away with
one sweep of his whispering eagle wing.

The Poet's Domain

Elaine Morgan

A rainbow filters through a crystal prism coloring his outer world. He's a child again, lying in a field of rattling corn stalks, eyes closed, watching colored lights. The moon waxes between his brows. He sings in his sleep and flies in his dreams. A one-eyed wounded healer waiting to take flight as a million winking stars light the hole in the sky and the floor of the earth.

He hears the scream of an eagle and realizes he is not alone. A Spirit flies the banner of itself, chanting a Shaman song. He does not hear himself sing. He does not hear himself sing. He whispers as softly as the wink of the eyelid of an owl. As gently as the flutter of the wing of a butterfly. He whispers like the sweep of the wing of an eagle as it takes flight.

Choose Something Like a Star

Sometimes during Summers . . .

Sometimes I remember times I spent with
Granddad Fred who wrote poetry and
read Bobby Burns and Robert Frost to
show who he thought were the best.

Always during summers, after I quit school for a while,
I'd go to South Charleston where he lived and
I'd sit in the swing on the porch while he
read and talked about life.

Extrordinary teacher, he taught me during
that time I decided to work instead.
He didn't say: "Go back to school you
fool," as Dad put it. Fred knew how hard-
headed grandkids could be.

Wise, Fred taught by example, reading his
own work. Good caring company he
showed his love by not "preaching" as
Dad did, with cuss words sprinkled in
between.

I still remember looking forward to those
weekend visits when Fred promised can-
taloupe and vanilla ice cream and Bobby
Burns and Robert Frost.

Lu Motley

is a graduate of the University of Louisville, and the University of Cincinnati. She also attended Virginia Commonwealth University where she received a certification in English. In her many incarnations Lu has been a soloist with several churches in Richmond, and has performed with the Virginia Museum Theater as Buttercup in *HMS Pinafore*, and Mrs. Peachum in *Threepenny Opera* as well as the farmer's wife in *Mother Courage*. Her play, *Mom and Min*, was performed in 1987 at Theater IV in Richmond. Lu is currently active with the Virginia Production Alliance.

Lu Motley

Teacher

Not inspired to write a damn,
I sit and ponder what I am,
Then, forlorn and sad I begin to wonder . . .

Could I frankly be mad?

After dealing with that thought for a while
I continue to go to assign students to
desks where they, bored and meek sit in
their little world where we consign them.

Sit there John, the hell with your experience.
Sit over there Mary, pretty little girl with
bright eyes!

Which express much delight later on . . .
though with kids today, how they move on!!

To grapple with life and spawn . . .

Little bits whose life goes faster,

they produce those who'll come one more
time to be assigned those same little desks
in those same classrooms in that same little
same old school.

To Frost

I'm still alive though some may disagree.
Why?
Why afraid?
Age doesn't set my gauge.
Rich memories bring much joy.

All I then had,
gives life more to love as never before.

Upon Viewing Albert Bierstadt's Mt. Corcoran

One doesn't need to have visited Mt. McKinley
or to have traveled to the Austrian Alps,
to marvel at Albert Bierstadt's Mt. Corcoran;
to see the green depths of the pond,
or to hear the low moan
of the wind in the giant firs,
to feel the cool mist of the clouds
and wonder at the size of the black bear
walking to the waters edge.

Like the black bear seeking water,
I search to quench my thirst
for more paintings of earth's grandeur.

Upon Viewing Monet's Water Lilies

On aqua pond
tinged with pink by the sun,
see how water lilies,
caught by the current,
float above grasses swaying.

Ruby Lee Norris is a retired secondary school educator whose specialty was teaching American literature, journalism, and humanities. She is member of the Chesapeake Bay Writers Club. For more than fifteen years she has been gardening columnist, photographer, and feature writer for *Pleasant Living Magazine*. In addition, she writes and photographs features for *Virginia Gardener* and *Bay Splash* magazines. Her poems have appeared in earlier issues of *The Poet's Domain*. She also writes short stories and vignettes about life on the Middle Peninsula.

Ruby Lee Norris

Through My Lens

I try to snap an instant,
try to catch a sun ray's blazing path,
as it walks across the water to the horizon
and leaps into the sun.

I try to catch devotion
in the clasp of our hands.
it blazes at our touch,
burns into memory.

I try to hold her smile,
try to return his wink,
I let them linger long after
we go our separate ways.

I try to master the moment
when we kneel to pray
surrounded by fellow worshippers
as "things unseen" slip by

like a soft summer breeze
that blows over our heads,
over our speaking, our thinking,
to surface any instant in infinity.

Cry

I have never forgotten what your arms feel like
I think this would be easier if I could
Imagine never being a part of love
A part of your circle or inner passion and desire
But with the distance comes a greater yearning
A fire with a flame that refuses to be quieted
In my solitude I reflect on every moment
I am at the core of your beating
I am at the center of your screaming
I dance within the rhythm of love
In the distance I sing
A lone she-wolf cry
A woman's mournful call for her mate to come home
And I stay up and circle the moon until it is way too late

Charlie Palumbo

has spent many hours writing poetry and journaling to keep her mind calm. She finds writing to be the perfect meditation. She has always loved writing, art, and music. Charlie enjoys sharing her words because she believes that someone may need them. She is mother, veteran, wife, poet, and friend. "I truly feel blessed on a daily basis, and I am thankful for the voice I have been given."

The Poet's Domain

Charlie Palumbo

The Wilds of a Woman

Wild
Women
Nature
Dog
Life
Characteristics
Misplaced
Longing
Obsession
Knowledge
Scared
Forgotten
Ugly
Terrible
Better
Everything
Forces
Us
To
Continue
Life
Death
Life
Cycle
Configuration
The
Phases
Of
Love

Choose Something Like a Star

Wild Flower

Some parents wish
their offspring
to be a rose
perfect in coloring,
genetics and pose.
Others prefer wild
flowers waving in the breeze
chasing sun rays
and doing as they please.
I'll always be grateful
to Mom and Dad
for nurturing free will
both good and bad;
for not stifling
my growth
with starched
lace and bows;
they instinctively
knew I wasn't a rose.

Instead, they allowed
this wild flower
to be
just plain
and simple,
little ole'
me.

Donna Harter Raab

lives in Fredericksburg, Virginia, with her husband, two children, their many pets, and numerous backyard squirrels and birds. Donna grew up on a small farm in Billings, Missouri, and graduated magna cum laude with a degree in communication from Missouri State University. She began her professional career as a copywriter and then a project manager and copywriter in advertising. In 1999 the family relocated to Virginia, and Donna began working at the University of Mary Washington, where today she is the senior director of advancement communications.

Donna Harter Raab

The Tornado

We put out food for the hummingbirds;
fed the Holstein calves, and then we heard;
the weatherman said it was coming fast;
the storm was a big one that would not pass.
He said to seek shelter and hunker down;
it was headed straight for my home town.
My sister, Mom, Dad, and me
ran to an inside room and hit our knees.
The sky turned green and trees were still;
we heard the noise and we could feel;
the fury of the storm held us down;
the house creaked, and the wind howled.
Glass broke, boards popped; we prayed
the monster would leave;
and the storm would abate.
What seemed like hours finally came to an end;
the tornado gave up and skipped round the bend.
We slowly stood and wondered when
the inside had gone out; the outside come in.
Everything was a shambles, a real mess;
we were alive and grateful, I guess.
The old barn was gone, calves were dead;
fences were missing along with the sheds.
The monstrous wind had reshaped the land;
trees were twisted and few could stand.
Our path to civilization now blocked;
vehicles mangled, and so I walked.
I crawled over trees to reach the road
to see more devastation there bestowed.
The jumbled world round me could not be;
nature's treasures had become debris.
I talked to a lawman from the county;
he was only there to do the counting.
He asked if anyone was dead; I said no;
he briskly swept past; I decided to go.

Choose Something Like a Star

Donna Harter Raab

I trudged back to the house;
it was still standing;
spied a canoe up a tree,
then heard a humming.
Two tiny birds alive
and searching for food;
one small miracle brightened
my solemn mood.

The Water Answers

It seems
whenever I'm in the mood
to think, theorize,
or simply brood,
I seek water
to clear my mind;
to help relax
and unwind.
Form or flow
doesn't seem to matter;
a river, a lake,
a body of water;
fountains,
ocean waves,
waterfalls;
wherever it is,
it always calls.

I'm not
alone
in this simple quest
for peace;
I've met others
just like
me.
They sit
and sigh

Donna Harter Raab

as they silently wait
for the swooshing
seas to signal
their fate.

"Swish,
gurgle,
blurp,"
the water answers.
"I am the song
and you
are the dancers.
Follow
my rhythm
and sing
to the wind;
wisdom,
peace,
and love,
I will
send.

You
are but a drop
in this sea of strife;
I am the power
and the giver
of life.
Toss me your troubles,
grave
or benign.
Reach through
the mist
to grasp
your
lifeline."

Choose Something Like a Star

Choosing Light

Destiny is not a matter of chance—it is a matter of choice. It is not a thing to be waited for—it is a thing to be achieved. —William Jennings Bryan

Weeks of wading through storm-tutored Spring,
jarred into silence by the loudness of pain,
old bones and souls beg for revision.
Their 2:00 A.M. mind belts itself
for flights to landscapes near and far.
Darkness is lively space for launching
fresh pictures of once and future sightings.

The hummers finally returned
to their feeders, five days past
faithful placement on April 15.
The birds rest upon a remembered branch
of the Kwansan Cherry tree. They tarried
yesterday to examine, close-up,
a bathrobe watching from a window.

Mr. Goose, a "come here" who lingers,
has been strolling aimlessly
at water's edge, banished from nesting
with Mrs. Goose with whom for weeks
he enjoyed salty sands, steep rocks,
young grasses on the greening lawn.

Outside in darkness skies are clearing,
so star-lights twinkle as if forever
and tempt sleepy eyes almost to dawn.
The whence and whither of visible light—
proxy of energies still out of sight—
have been studied by scientists for lifetimes

Robert A. Rickard

is a retired federal executive who lives and writes on Capitol Hill, in Washington, D.C. and at Laetare, his home in the Northern Neck of Virginia. His work appeared in the Poetry Society of Virginia's *80th Anniversary Anthology of Poems*. This is the eighth appearance of his poetry in *The Poet's Domain*.

The Poet's Domain

Robert A. Rickard

since Galileo. They say life depends
on light, that life scattered across a planet
circling its Sun, on a spiral arm
whirling 'round a milky-starred galaxy.

Some scientists say nothing is forever,
concluding the universe is finite.
But naming and dating the orbs continues
deep into mysteries of starry sky.
Should their Sun, in its fate, disappear,
migrant life will have peopled new worlds,
like feathered friends bridging the seasons.
Life loves the light and chooses it forever.

Choose Something Like a Star

The Companions

Riotous hours,
endless waves,
tossing tides
of time

Navigating
unsettled night
I reign above,
quietly alone
stoic sentry
mourning the days,
now shadows of centuries

Forgiving of
my cool condescension
uneven reflection,
multitudes wink and flirt
precocious ones
parade around,
beam and fade

Heavenly friends, the stars,
welcome companions
to this crusty old man

Dawn Riddle

was born in 1967, and raised with her identical twin in Portsmouth, Virginia. She earned her undergraduate and graduate degrees in sociology at Virginia colleges: Mary Washington and William & Mary, respectively. Ms. Riddle currently manages the *Mansion on Main* Bed & Breakfast in Smithfield, Virginia; and enjoys hosting the Isle of Wight writers' group there.

Tom Russell

is a retired administrative librarian and a graduate of Kenyon College and of the University of Michigan. He studied with J. C. Ransom, John Ciardi, William Packard, and Ann Darr. His work appears in volumes 8, 11–14, 16, 20–25 of *The Poet's Domain*. Published in a number of other magazines and anthologies, he has given readings in seven states. A former officer of the Poetry Society of Virginia, he resides in Harrisonburg, Va.

Erasmus Darwin's Grandson Wrote of the Descent of Man, St. Francis

and it's a heady thing
looking across
billions of star-years
of carbo amino acidic ascent
of this spine and brain
conscious of being
conscious and of the process
collectively to flow together and concelebrate
individually to return to cosmic stardust and
how fortunate to wonder grounded where I am
in these extraordinary successivenesses.

St. Francis, Perfection

Thoughts sputter in the sacristy of the mind
unable to reach full flame as some at the altar.

Consider the rate of motion without mass
or a stream of sound penetrating solid light.

I am become whatever lies at the limits
of my inadequacies. Perfection need not seek.

Draped in alb and stole but unhidden
costume hardly ensures the unction of very truth.

Could that speed with no mass be of Him
and those chips of solid light across the sky?

Choose Something Like a Star

Fears Allayed

How quiet, solid, big he always seemed.
My fear? He wished a son instead of me.
My mother chided, said he never dreamed.
My fear? He visioned them of daughter free.

When Mother left, this daughter went with her.
I saw him seldom, found him silent still.
Not father, daughter made overt demur.
At such communication, both lacked skill.

He married, had new children—girl and *boy*.
My relatives claim she and I are twinned.
The son, they say, has brought my dad scant joy.
I find that I am nothing but chagrined.

But I was pleased to hear this last report:
Dad's recollections? Times as *my* escort.

Lemurs and Other Spirits of the Madagascar Dead

Diégo Diaz, searching for a port
of call upon the spice route, chanced to land
at Nosy Be, went in with his cohort.
They found this strand as strange as
Samarkand.

Beyond their campfire all that long dark night,
they were beset by great bright eyes and howls.
Those peering eyes seemed sharp enough to bite!
His men ran mad from fear despite his scowls.

Lynn Veach Sadler

A former college president in Vermont, Dr. Lynn Veach Sadler has published widely in academics and creative writing (including a novella, short-story collection, chapbooks, and forthcoming novel and poetry book). One story appears in *Del Sol's Best of 2004 Butler Prize Anthology*; another won the 2006 *Abroad Writers* Contest/Fellowship (France). She was named 2007 Writer of the Year by California's *elizaPress* and won the 2008 Pearson Award at Wayne State for a play on the Iraq wars. A play on Frost was a *Pinter Review* Prize for Drama Silver Medalist.

Lynn Veach Sadler

They named the lemurs "spirits of the dead."
Those Europeans missed the missing link—
ancestors are the dead who walk instead.
The living from the dead there never shrink.

Each year, the bodies of the dead are raised,
re-clothed, and cleansed, their sacred worms released
to grow to giant snakes that thus are praised.
Were they the cause Diaz's men decreased?

Guideposts

My father's quietness—
a matter of dignity
rather than a deliberate withholding
of himself from his wife and daughter.
Always thinking of how to better
what we were, what we had.
My mother's measure,
sweet reasonableness,
pre-planning, detail.

Aunt Lou Ellen, silly maybe,
but blossoming into an object
of some pity, admiration
for the bigness of her pettiness
in her chase after motes of dust.

Uncle Jim, always beloved,
but much pitied for
the nagging wife who drove him
to while away his time
with captive listeners.

Choose Something Like a Star

Lynn Veach Sadler

Old Willie Kenan,
who would drink all night
but still manage to swab and turn
a whole pig cooked over
a bed of coals on a mesh frame
at one of our tobacco barns
so that we could all,
tenant and boss-family,
White and Black,
feast the next day.

The cold, wet slap in my face
of the morning's
first hands of green tobacco
because I was the littlest,
had to take the middle of
one side of the tobacco truck
between two adults.

The string art Hezzie and Mattie Lou
tried to teach me on the rare occasions
the barn hands emptied a truck
before the boy brought
the next load of tobacco from the field.

A new outfit for Easter,
even if it was a dress.
The one I ruined riding a goat.

The opening of the eyes of a baby squirrel
the logging crew brought in
from the woods for me.
A myriad of pets.

A myriad of peeks
at what life could be.

Lynn Veach Sadler

Here's to the New Philistines

Here's to the New Philistines,
the New Helmsmen bestriding land,
bestriding mind,
keeping lights under bushels,
nailing those bushels down.
They won't let our marvels—marvelous out.

The Yahoos abound—at all levels,
grow in the dark; convert, happily,
*like*mind to *light*mind.
(We've dismissed them as
mere trouble with tribbles.)
Do they think they also glow?
They curse the light, don't die.

While we've slouched toward Bethlehem,
dabbled daintily at Helicons,
smiled pleasantly
at oh-so-pretty gonfalons,
patted the heads of polite myrmidons,
they've manicured mayhem,
exuded strong negative energy, brute raw power.
Anarchy and Culture are yet in conflict.
Culture never seems to know it.
Does Culture perchance have
too much sweetness and not enough light?

We query whether eggs are to be broken
at big or small ends, are to be broken at all;
question which way toilet paper unrolls;
extract sunshine from cucumbers;
wax precious in the convolutions
of "making one's way."
It's enough to make one "Neigh!"
and turn Houyhnhnm,
join Light-Horse Harry Lee's Legion.

Choose Something Like a Star

Lynn Veach Sadler

Our writers knew, wrote
the light may go out before August.
Can it keep Joe alive for Christmas?
Nat Turner was troubled by August's blue lights.
The light that was the Princess Casamassima—
the same light that's failed?

Don't let the *lower* lights be burning.
They're *not* the lights upon the shore.

How long has it been
since a Lincoln read by candle-, firelight?
How long has it been since a Lincoln *read*?
Since a Lincoln *was*?

We *can* trim our wicks, brighten *up*.
When? Be swift!
I've turned *Whenhnhnm*,
no matter how much I love Swift.

The Promise Recanted

Early morning the sky is grey, lumbering,
the promised snow imminent.
In the store shoppers fill their carts
with loaves of bread, milk,
the stuff of soups and hearty fare
appropriate to a fire and weekend television.
Their faces wizened by the need to rush,
the urgency of icy roads
graying their minds despite the now blue skies.

By evening, the snow has yet to fall.
Our lives still graceless, flawed, and though
the sky is cloudless, the stars crystalline,
such resplendence cannot assuage our need—
the air cleansed of soot,
rubble subsumed into a whitened whole,
the world made pure,
Eden reclaimed.

Lynda Self

has published poetry previously in *The Threepenny Review, The Southern Review, The New England Review, The Georgia Review,* and *Confrontation.* Three of these poems were anthologized in the *Yearbook of American Poetry* (1981, 1984, and 1985). A number of her poems appeared in *The Poet's Domain* (volumes 2, 7, and 9). A recent poem appears in the winter 2008 issue of the *Southern Humanities Review*; another will appear in a forthcoming issue of the *Southern Poetry Review.* Lynda now resides in Waynesville, North Carolina.

Lynda Self

Late Summer

On rainy days the mountains recede
    behind the hovering mist,
impenetrable and gray.
Now in late summer, the trees themselves
obscure the view,
their leaves a curtain of green.
From the deck where the view is best,
I sit afternoons and read or watch the birds,
eyes asquint against the still bright sun.
Today the birds seem almost absent
    except I hear in the trees
the insistent che-weet of goldfinches and
    occasionally a crow's cry.

Late summer is a leaden time, the air itself
    grown still—
stirred only by the insects' noiseless flight.
I wait for fall—for the descent of leaves and
    an unobstructed view of distant heights.
Stillness displaced by drafts of wind
    as the trees fade into foreground, yielding
the mountains their proper stead:
    the obdurate stone
not challenge but succor.

The Poet's Domain

Shirley Nesbit Sellers

is a retired teacher of Norfolk public schools and resides in Norfolk where she is active in storytelling and in workshops of poetry writing and storytelling. Past president of the Poetry Society of Virginia, she has won numerous awards in the Society, the Irene Leache Memorial Contests, and was second place winner of the 1997 Poetry Manuscript Contest of the National Federation of State Poetry Societies for her manuscript, *Winds from the Bay*. She has published a chapbook, *Where the Gulls Nest: Norfolk Poems*, published by Ink Drop Press.

December Windows

The holly and berry,
sun bright green and cheery
bring nearly starved robins to sills in the snow.
The high drifts the flow makes
from wind driven snowflakes
are white lakes within the bright windowpanes'
glow.
Across the high skylight
pass sunlight and twilight,
and stars become icebreakers on the dark seas.
All night, frozen twig trickles
make shining icicles,
tinkling and tickling the glass from the trees.
Inside, glowing log glimmers,
candlelight star shimmers,
and bright eyes reflecting the windowpanes'
fires,
draw closer the yuletide
from inside and outside
to lighten all yearnings and year-end desires.

Starlight

I stand still and watch
as the high bridge lights compete
with the twilight stars.
Now, with Father Moon,
each challenges its siblings in a sparkle race.
In vain, Mother Cloud blankets
her children for bed.
They just laugh and glow.

Shirley Nesbit Sellers

Wartime Goodbye

I'll never forget the day that we met
when the world seemed to change for me,
and that first gay dance where we found romance
that grew with each melody.
I'll remember, too, 'neath a sky of blue
the days spent on the shore,
the friendship and fun—unreal life just begun
that I'd never known before.
I'll remember those nights when the soft
bridge lights
crossed the river in silvery bars,
how you held my hand and the things that
    we planned
as we stood in the spell of the stars.
The stars and I know that you said you must go,
but that you would return, would be true,
that our dreams must not die with a spoken
    goodbye.
I'll remember it all—will you?

The Poet's Domain

Ann Falcone Shalaski

was born in Connecticut and lives in Newport News, Va. Ann is a member of the National League of American Pen Women, the Poetry Society of Virginia, and president of the advisory council for Christopher Newport University's Writers' Conference. Her work has appeared in *The Comstock Review, Main Channel Voices, Port Folio Weekly, ByLine*, and numerous other publications. Her debut poetry collection, *World Made of Glass*, was published recently by San Francisco Bay Press.

Center of the Universe

People are content on Pleasant Street.
Stand or lean from narrow porch railings
white as doilies.
Children run baselines, moon lifts over
the courthouse clock, and every evening,
the bread trucks pass.

Summer going faster than it came,
I forged a trail between the clapboard houses,
buried a map in a field growing still.
With a wave of my hand, I'd point to a perfect
spot. Lines fanning out, twisting, turning me
far from the life I was destined to live.

Only the dark knew my secret.
Now, so little seems so right.
Fields behind the house, sidewalk where I wrote
my name. Children playing on the front porch
steps, shadows growing larger, longer
every year. Summer sky opening with stars.

Ann Falcone Shalaski

Falling Back into Life

Happy late in life,
they're not afraid to let the quiet in
or mix living with dying.

There's hushed talk of what they'll find
on the other side, who will be there
to lift them over the threshold.

That it's best to give everything away now,
her demitasse cups, his silver pocket watch.
How little it all comes to.

Patiently arranging pansies in clay pots,
beneath clouds shaped like blossoms
bursting into the unknown,

they fall back into life again, edge
the garden path with simple stones.
Knowing, little else matters except

this familiar ground of home,
and the end that they see
so clearly.

Hope

shepherds us through gray spirals,
where dreams cover the landscape

like slivers of moon, a thin peel of soap
we hold in our hands.

Ann Falcone Shalaski

Family Matters

Body pared down to a thread,
she snaps at the suggestion
of leaving her home.

We are children at the kitchen table.
Listening as she struggles to turn thoughts
into words, words into meaning that floats

beyond her grasp like years.
She lived so long in this house
next to the bakery,

she knew where everything was,
life laid out like a road map.
Now, mother's face is lined with living.

Each day poses more questions,
a mystery for her to unravel like tangled
geraniums on the sill thick with dust.

Empty bottles of pills, food she's forgotten
how to prepare. Hands flutter in the air
like little veined petals;

she denies our presence, the end that's come.
Retreats to a space so small, so impossible,
not even love can find her.

While Dancing
An ekphrastic interpretation of Pierre-Auguste Renoir's A Dance in the Country (1841–1919)

She wears a broad smile
One hand rests on her partner's shoulder
The other holds his hand and a fancy fan
A red bonnet tied under her chin
Adorned in a flowery flowing
Bustled evening gown
With ruffled bottom
Her dark bearded partner's
Profiled nose leans in
To breathe in aromas
Of her perfumed flaming red hair
Is she smiling because of her partner
Or flirting with someone else's dance partner

Barbara Drucker Smith

is a regional, national anthologized poet, fiction, nonfiction writer, author of *Darling Loraine, The Story of A. Louis Drucker: A Grateful Jewish Immigrant, A Poetic Journey, Prose from the Old Century to the New: Vignettes, Petite Petites, Epistles, Points of View*—all nominated for the Library of Virginia Awards. The Barbara Smith GNU Writers Fund provides awards and enables top writers for talks and workshops.

Lila

Children playing hide and seek
Place themselves in situations from which
they must escape
Why do they do so
When they could free themselves by simply
withdrawing
From the game?

Maybe the game is its own reward?
In some mysterious way, maybe it is the world?
Like a child playing alone
God is the cosmic dancer
Whose routine is all dancers and all worlds.

From the tireless stream
Divine energy
The cosmos
Flows in endless
Graceful reenactment

George Stietz

is a beatnik. Just like fellow beat poets, Ginsberg and Kerouac, Stietz writes of Buddhist tendencies and the Dharma ways. He honed his craft putting in late nights, huddled over his espresso at the Gaslight cafe, and was no stranger to draping his arms over fellow beat poets for photos at City Lights Books. Days of yore were spent exploring the mind of some gone gal or parking cars or working some other bread job in some God-knows-where town. In between racing from coast to coast in search of mad adventure, Stietz earned a BSGA from Christopher Newport University and attended law school in Miami, Florida. Write him at: gstietz@yahoo.com.

Choose Something Like a Star

Constellation

the little
space

between is
but the twinkling
of a lie

for stars are far
apart, yet ever
fixed, mark

what out of memory
remains.

(constant love will
dip and die
before the
spinning star,

immune to hope
and pain.)

sunset haiku

the dissolving sun
makes a desert of the sky—
dunes, red and golden.

desolation waits
to make a seamless, silent
Universe of night.

H. Anne Stratford

currently resides in northeast Pennsylvania, but has more frequently been a resident of Ohio, Virginia, and Nevada. Her poems focus on the perseverance of the natural world. She often misses the clear night sky over the open desert.

H. Anne Stratford

Orison

the beauty of the night is sung
by stars in haunting orison,

the terror of the night revealed
in dark and shifting pathos.

on destiny the stars were hung,
by miles of silken wires were strung,

the fate of every soul concealed
in blinding light or shadow.

Choose Something Like a Star

When I Lose Count

As numbers merge like
Rainbow bands slipping
On the heels of thunderheads

My balance rests
Not in being unfazed
By tipping, toppling tugs

But in loosening the reins
In factoring the me
I rarely see

I count on her

Mary Talley

was born in Waco, Texas, and after living in Oklahoma, Belgian Congo, Richmond, D.C., and Hatteras Island, now lives in Virginia Beach. She enjoys low-key gardening, spoiling cats, water volleyball, duplicate bridge, and good humor. Her poems have recently appeared in *The Poet's Domain.*

The Poet's Domain

Lesley M. Tyson

was born in Toronto, Canada of English parents; spent her childhood in upstate New York and "came of age" in Houston, Texas, settling in the Virginia suburbs after graduating college. She has had work published in issues of *The Poet's Domain* and other D.C. Metro area local publications (*Spiraeas, Poetry Just for You*). Lesley also participated in the 2005 and 2008 Poets and Painters exhibits in Northern Virginia. She is a co-author of *Can You Come Here Where I Am?*, an anthology of writings by breast cancer survivors. Lesley is a regular contributor to several local Northern Virginia poetry groups.

question a star

you will not find your dreams
hanging a weak light in the night sky
there is no hidden treasure
in the star trapped in your gaze
even if it could would it reveal
the answers lay out a plan
the star just shines
a small light against the dark
burning consuming itself as fuel
maybe this is the lesson
you must expend yourself to be
and by being become your own light

control the night

to avoid thinking too much
i cut light to pieces
like strips of paper
like broken doors
like shadows under my shoe
i reduced the views
to smaller and smaller pieces
that were more bearable
easier to fold
fit into boxes
shut into drawers
hide under shadows
so light was reduced
locked away
night asserted control
dreams shifted thoughts
into probabilities calculated by
the mathematics of starlight

Choose Something Like a Star

Lesley M. Tyson

something like a star

your studied alchemy
read all the texts ancient and modern
practiced each art experimented with each science
you pored over works of late masters
and attended the lectures of present experts
with all your learning you forgot to feel
and don't comprehend matters of the heart
i can give you no accolades
you are like a bright evening star
beautiful but providing nothing
no answers to the eternal why
yet perhaps you are something like a star
remote emotionless untouchable
giving only a weak flickering light
barely enough to mark a path

star-crossed

is it different words
with the same meaning
these dreams we both want
is it separate paths
to the same destination
or do we follow
stars in separate skies

The Poet's Domain

Lesley M. Tyson

hope upon a star

why should these pinpricks of light
on the wall of night
have a greater language
than the messages we create
why should they possess
answers to questions
we cannot leave unresolved
hopefully we believe the stars
watch us with the same wonder
not willing to accept
we are invisibly small
on a tiny blue planet
hardly visible against
the dark day of the universe

Choose Something Like a Star

The Miracle of Birth: Orion, Nursery for the Stars

All births are a miracle
Unrivaled by the first creation.
No less a miracle is the birthing of stars
In the process of death
And transformation of suns.
They are the source of all matter,
Creating clouds of gas and dust,
Then collapsing into black holes
Sucking in all matter and even light within
their cosmic force.
In the iron laws of the Cosmos
The Great Watchmaker has decreed
That nothing is gained or lost
But constantly reincarnated into new forms
And matter to energy.
Energy into light—Light illuminating the
Great and Ghastly Blackness.

The Orion nebula is a nursery for the stars.
With Betelgeuse and Bellatrix for shoulders.
In his manhood lives the Orion nebula
Growing red in creative flame
With the energy of reproduction.

Star dust collapses
Into new stars and plumes and planets
In the Trapezium heart of the bowl-shaped
Nebula,
With blue and green and yellow
An unfolding of gas and dust
Completing the eternal cycle of
Death and birth and resurrection.

Jack Underhill

has a Ph.D. from George Mason University in public policy (1995), a masters in public administration from the Kennedy School of Government at Harvard (1969), a masters in public law and government from Columbia University (1959), a bachelor's degree in international relations from University of California at Berkeley (1954). He is self-taught in photography, art, wood sculpture, and poetry. He is the father of three children and grandfather of seven grandchildren. He is the author of books on American, Soviet, and French new towns. He has had a number of poems published.

The Poet's Domain

Jack Underhill

Is there one God for all these galaxies,
Or many gods
Or are we alone,
The sole living creatures with souls
In the entire Universe
Spinning and surging on a solo journey through
The black lifeless freezing void
With no one to talk to but ourselves?

An Ominous Black Hole in the Sky

In the center of our modest galaxy,
One of 100 billion known or suspected in
the Universe,
Is a deep mystery:
A black hole
Four million times the mass of our sun
From which no light,
Not even thought or hope, can escape.

Around this one-eyed monster
Swim a great cluster of stars
Like a hive of hot bees.
Stars captured for eternity in the center
Hurry frantically
At twenty million miles an hour.
Hot gas is sucked into the hole
Never to be seen again.

This unseen presence creates a funnel
Distorting the fabric of space itself.
The deeper the whirlpool,
       the faster the stars swirl.

Choose Something Like a Star

Jack Underhill

What future events lurk
For this unfriendly monster?
Another galaxy, Andromeda, is on a
Collision course with our own Milky Way.
Massive black holes may collide
Two billion years from now
Igniting a new quasar in our
Serene corner of the universe.

Fireworks!

Waiting for the Foxes

There is a stillness
before the dawn fingers paint the sky,
when the shrill barking of the foxes begins.
Once in the mountains,
I heard one close by,
looked out and saw his furry form against
the pines.
He was silent then,
as if he knew I listened,
waiting for him to begin again,
calling to his mate perhaps
or to furry babies in the den.

My foxes are in a picture
on the kitchen wall.
One head rests upon the other,
eyes closed peacefully in sleep.
There's a redness of the fur
bits of white marking the ears and jaws,
two noses black as coal,
the whiskers long and white.
I imagine my foxes
barking in the dawn,
leaping and cavorting,
free as the mountain wind.

Elizabeth Urquhart

was born in Colorado and grew up in New Mexico. Many of her poems are about the Southwest. She studied English literature and history at the University of Iowa and later earned a master's degree at Old Dominion University in Norfolk, Va. Elizabeth writes poetry and is interested in gardening, music, and wildlife. Her three children now grown and scattered, she lives with her computer scientist husband and two cats in Hampton, Va. She is a member of the Williamsburg Poetry Guild and the Poetry Society of Virginia. Her poetry has appeared in six previous volumes of *The Poet's Domain*.

Elizabeth Urquhart

Geronimo

I am Geronimo, Apache chieftain,
once known as Gauathlay (one who yawns)

The rag around my head is red,
the color of the blood
that my people sacrificed for their freedom.
Their bones lie whitened, by the sun,
On mounds of desert earth.

We were placed on the Reservation by our conquerors,
Told to live the white man's life,
To learn his language, worship his God.
We left the Reservation.

Under the midnight cloak of darkness,
my band and I rode our horses
over the border into Mexico.
We attacked the villages of poor peasants;
Stole horses, sheep, and slaves.

We were captured then by the general
and forced to surrender.
Now, we ride the steam horse to a distant land.
White Eyes tells us what to do.
My men call me traitor,
They say we should have fled.

We're older now.
My wife is dying of the coughing sickness.
My child will die as well.
Our hearts are heavy, the sky is black,
Our desert and mountains have gone.

Perhaps the white man's God will let us live awhile,
They say he is a merciful God.
I am Geronimo, Apache chieftain.

Elizabeth Urquhart

Cinco de Mayo

The mestizo,
crimson scarf waving,
gallops his caballo
over sagebrush and cactus,
down sharp canyons,
across rushing streams,
towards Puebla.
Sharp machete
tied to the saddle,
worn sombrero
hanging by a string.
His country is in danger,
the French threaten.
Miguel leaves wife
and small child,
to ride the spotted
hard breathing Estrella
to victory.

The Navajo Code Talkers

Dooley Shorty, Navajo, 88 years old, died
last week.
He trained Navajo code talkers for World
War II.
The code talkers used their language to
confuse and frustrate
the Japanese, who never deciphered it.
Dooley, born in Cornfield, Arizona wore a
large black hat
with silver conchos, a sky-blue turquoise
necklace
and taught silversmithing for 30 years.
During the war, the young Navajo men
radioed

Choose Something Like a Star

Elizabeth Urquhart

their words to describe military equipment.
Tas-chizzie, Navajo for swallow, meant torpedo plane;
jay sho, buzzard, was bomber;
dahe-tih-hi, hummingbird, meant fighter plane.
Iwo Jima and other South Pacific battles were won
with the code talkers' aid.

Paul Edward Tso said, "I was afraid of nothing.
I felt that if I was going to end my life in war,
that was the way it should be."
Thomas Begay, who was awarded six battle stars said,
"I believe in the traditional Navajo ways.
I felt that the great spirit was protecting me.
My parents had ceremonies to keep me safe."
Dan Akee, of the 4th Marine Division, said,
"The war was very sad.
I saw dead marines on the beach of Iwo Jima.
We had to go through them."

The proud and brave Navajo word warriors
came out of the mesas and Southwestern mountains
to serve their country with love and pride.
A country that once had broken treaties
and tried to crush the Dineh—the people.

The Poet's Domain

Elizabeth Urquhart

Sara Swifthawk

Sara Swifthawk in faded brown moccasins
walks three miles to Oljato trading post
—Place of the Moonlight Water.
The frost is heavy the cold bites,
her turquoise and silver jewelry is to be
pawned for food.
Sara Swifthawk, jet hair sprinkled with white,
face a network of wrinkles, needs food more
than fuel.

The trader smiles kindly as he gives her
canned peaches and beans.
Sara walks home slowly.
She builds a fire of piñon logs,
puts on a kettle of beans to cook,
then settles down in a warm blanket.

Sara Swifthawk passes into a dream world
bright with desert flowers that lift the heart
and spirit.
When she was young, she herded sheep in
canyons and mesas.
She danced the squaw dance with young
men who gave her money.
She rode her palomino pony to sings where
she was allowed to chant.
Sam Begay, Sara's husband, married into
her clan of many waters.
She gave birth to three children; all of whom
have left the reservation.
Sam Begay died some years ago of the
hanta virus sickness.
Now, Sara Swifthawk lives by herself.
She gathers yucca with which to wash her hair.
She weaves colorful rugs to sell.

Elizabeth Urquhart

The harshness of winter has surrounded her.
Sara Swifthawk is too weak to gather more wood.
Sara now in her dream, rides her pony
across an arroyo.
She hears the desert owl, small and lively in
his cactus nest.
The cold wraps around her,
She is spirited away.

Properties of Tapioca

Murk can be a shape
risen piled made
beyond cobweb,
while a dot of distance
shines
like a coin
found in the last place.

It may just happen
along all tries
in the moment: diving
for pearls, fishing
with a stone, gathering
a star
until it makes a hole.

And even when the tool
works, sometimes time is
the matter,
sending everything else
over the cliff
to land
like pudding.

Douglas Alan Wandersee

earned a bachelor of arts at the University of Minnesota-Morris in 1993 and master of education at James Madison University in 1999. He lives in the Shenandoah Valley, working at Eastern Mennonite University and WMRA public radio.

Choose Something Like a Star

Looking Up

I loved the summer twilights when my father
took me strolling along beside the sea,
my small hand held in his wide, strong one,
short legs struggling to match his stride.

It was past my bedtime but we didn't care.
The ripe red moon swam up out of the ocean,
turned paler as it climbed the evening sky.
Then the stars began to twinkle.

My father tried to make me see the star-shapes:
Orion's Belt, the Bear, and the Big Dipper.
He told how ancient men once sailed
uncharted seas
with only stars to guide them.

Though I squinted, peered, and tried,
I never really saw those mythic shapes.
To me the stars were pinholes in a great
black blanket
thrown across the sky to hide the splendor
just above.

If only I could see more clearly through the
star holes
I thought I'd catch a glimpse of Paradise aglow.
I never could.
But walking with my father in the evening
was heaven enough for me.

Edith White

(b. 1923, Passaic, N.J.) Storyteller, water color painter, book reviewer, librarian, teacher. Graduated from Vassar College. Served two years as Lt.jg in the U.S. Navy. Married Dr. Forrest P. White, pediatrician. Has four chldren, eight grandchildren, and has lived in Norfolk over fifty years. A member of the Poetry Society of Virginia, her work has appeared in many volumes of *The Poet's Domain*.

The Poet's Domain

Edith White

Stardust Universe

I stretch out on a grassy slope
to gaze into the night.
The rising moon, tomato red,
fills me with delight.

Nothing I see except the moon
in black and silent sky,
but I know that myriad wonders
are hidden from my eye.

How many are the galaxies
in outer realms now gliding
with suns and stars so wide apart
there's no fear of colliding?

It may be there are planets
within our universe
where creatures are developing
in countless forms diverse.

The universe expanding
extends in space so far.
Aeons of light years stretch out
beyond our palest star.

Experts search the distant skies
through powerful telecopes.
Scientists probe minutiae with
electron microscopes.

So much has been discovered
on this planet we call home.
We begin to grasp in wonder
how much is still unknown.

Edith White

Since all are made of stardust;
atom, human, galaxy, and quark,
must we all continue spinning
forever in the dark?

An Evening in May

Light rain at twilight.
Air so moist and fragrant
it could fill
        a long-stemmed
        crystal flute.
Tip it.
Sip it.
        Toast the starfilled night

The Poet's Domain

Edith White

Preserves

When we used to visit Grandma at her farm
sometimes she let me go down the cellar with her
to fetch a treat for dinner.
In her cool, dark pantry closet there were shelves
lined with gleaming jars of luscious fruit preserve:
pears, peaches, cherries, figs, strawberry jam,
chutney, and watermelon pickle.

But best of all,
way out back behind the barn
I found an old stone well long out of use.
No rope nor bucket to let down,
but I could see dark water glinting
far below.
One clear day I squatted by the mossy hole
Peered down until I could see plainly
three bright stars preserved
in that dark liquid, fresh and chill.
Though Grandma and her house are lost to me,
for all I know
her three bright stars are down there still.

Choose Something Like a Star

Beauty

I see a butterfly eating her breakfast.
Beautiful. Serene. At peace.
Her joy fills my heart
As I listen to her song,
A song hidden somewhere in the breeze.
I long to catch what my eyes beheld,
To frame the beauty,
The peace. The joy. The love.
I sit on a nearby bench
And reach out to hold what I see.
Gratitude filling my being
I let go of what cannot be held,
This sacrament for those who see beauty
Along life's joyful journey.

Waiting New Life

Dampness beneath my sandy feet
Feeling the pulse of the sea
New life hidden in the moment
Waiting eagerly to be free
Remembering the pain that is ever present
Long before the joy comes
I befriend my sorrow
When I open myself to new visions
With dry stick in hand
Watching life burst forth from the sea
What appeared dead in me
Lifts its head and sings.
There is no death, no end
All is beginning, all is eternal.

Louise B. Wilson was educated at Westtown Secondary School and Guilford College; later founded Virginia Beach Friends (Quaker) Meeting, followed by the Virginia Beach Friends School. In 1960 she was named First Citizen of the Year in Virginia Beach, Virginia. Throughout her life she has written articles and short stories for the joy of writing.

Robert E. Young

is a retired social worker, medical school professor, and psychotherapist. He has taught at Bryn Mawr, University of Pennsylvania, VCU, Norfolk State, ODU, and from 1973 to 1991, at the Eastern Virginia Medical School in the Department of Psychiatry. He and his wife enjoy visits with their five children and two grandchildren. He does volunteer community work in conflict resolution and war resistance, writes poetry and short stories, and enjoys basketball, body surfing, yoga, theater, and meditation.

evermore

there once was a poet named poe
morbid at tell and at show
how he did such a job
presenting the macabre
masques more than we ever dare know.

Vincent's Bedroom at Arles, 1888

gauguin is gone. i am alone
within my yellow house
inside my dreams inside my skin
many will someday know
my longing for the beloved
oh, God, where is thy peace?
i thought the room
would somehow make it so

The brush-strokes of my palette
with color thick ablaze
besiege the empty room
portrait of my sweet young muse
eugene, no longer wont to bless
peers down into
pine coffin of my bed.

The shrinking walls
suck at shackled space,
looking glass sneers darkly at my soul
the window frames
charred by raven storms
through leaden eyes
the townsfolk jaw about my ear.

Choose Something Like a Star

Robert E. Young

Floorboards gnaw at purple veins
and leech my blood
into the cover of the bed
smeared with bile green
my father's empty chairs
an unused towel hangs limp.

Two blue doors
reflect the lyric of a starry night
the mystery of my eyes,
yet open to a tortured trail

beyond.

Advice: The Lost and the Found
A poem should not mean but be.
—Archibald MacLeish

If you would know a poem
do not be so erudite
get rid of the mind—
that guy studying the words

Just dance with it a little
let it ooze through your bones
forget you everything
you learned about poesy

Be lovers
get lost
pray
that you won't get found.

The Poet's Domain

Robert E. Young

Rheumy

Without even looking,
I found a four-leaf clover
this morning, Memorial Day, in my front yard—
amidst the dandelions, crab grass,
and Southern Belle fescue.
Jumped right out at me.
Reminded me of basic training
Camp Pickett, Virginia.
"All I wanna see is assholes and elbows,"
Sgt. Renko bellowed.
I was close by Eddie Johnson, quiet,
gentle, tow-haired kid from Wilmar,
Minnesota.
"The kind of kid that wins wars," the CO
said.

We were "policing the area" in this sorry
field of ragtag goldenrod.
Eddie kept pulling up four-leaf clovers.
"Where? Where?" I kept whimpering,
being citified, and rheumy-eyed in all this.
He'd just mumble, keeping real close to the
ground,
like Renko wanted, "There. There's one."
Along with some old Coke bottles, used-up
Trojans,
and four Tru-Flite golf balls,
he must've picked seven or eight of them.
Gave me one for good luck.
All these years I've been looking for one of
my own.
Never found it 'til now.

Eddie . . . he got his brains blown out in
Korea.
We won the war.

Choose Something Like a Star

Being Not Doing

I am leaf
of a thousand plants.

I know the sunlight
of the equinox
and the taste
of saltwater on my vines.

I have heard the jolt
of snowflakes on my stem
and the sound of photosynthesis
in June.

I travel to the nether world
and back
on the vitality
of your dreams.

I will find you
and fulfill you
with energy of growth
until you are terminal.

Ethereal Friend

The strength of your energy
is as solid as the voice
of a tectonic plate
as it caresses life.

You stand firm
and when need be
you are as soft
as a willow in a morning mist.

Steven Zimmerman

was born in 1942, Fort Wayne, Indiana; father of two emancipated children; Vietnam veteran, U.S. Army; spent thirty-seven years in the corporate world in the area of finance and risk management, and is now pursuing life from the other half of his brain.

Steven Zimmerman

My battered spirit
draws renewal
from the knowledge
of your constantly bending
rigidity.

You nudge me
to excellence
and restore my
hollow spaces.

My journey
is wholeness
with you as my side by.

Plucking Comets

As I search
for the Red Horizon
I will wander
purposefully.

My journey is begun.

While bathing yourself
in the silence of loneliness,
are you going to continue your search
for the corners
on the circle of life
as you wait for yesterday?

Or, will you pluck comets
from the Milky Way
with me?

Choose Something Like a Star

A Starbucks' Moment

On the way to do God's work,
I pause at my favorite Starbucks'
Morning "pub," faithfully clutching
My tall cappuccino, double shot,
In company of tenacious regulars
Of that unique Starbucks' community,
To meditate over what's ahead
Even as I learn to separate,
Watching America in all its diversity
Unable to match Starbucks' variety.

Flight's Joy

She kept massaging him on the flight
From Rochester to New York,
Soothing his unseen aches, consoling with
A penetrating touch and a fulfilled smile,
Till they both fell asleep.
Fortunate they were, the receiver
and the giver.
I rejoiced with them.

Hanan, My Iraqi Sister

Your bandaged face hiding
the pain of disfigurement
of a wounded seventeen-year old,
pretty as the girl next door,
begging with loving parents
the American soldiers to be
treated, please, she utters a
"thank you" penetrating like a
bomb my skin.

Rabbi Israel Zoberman was born in Chu, Kazakhstan, U.S.S.R.; ordained as a reform rabbi by the Hebrew Union College-Jewish Institute of Religion in 1974, has been founding rabbi to Congregation Beth Chaverim in Virginia Beach, Va., since 1985. He studied at the University of Illinois and McCormick Theological Seminary (the only rabbi to receive a doctor of ministry in pastoral care and counseling from this Presbyterian institution). His poetry and his translations from Hebrew have been published in *CCAR Journal*, *Poetica*, the *Jewish Spectator*, the *American Rabbi*, *Moment*, and *The Poet's Domain*, volumes 5 through 24.

Hanan, My Iraqi Sister won first place in the 2008 Cenie H. Moon Prize Contest sponsored by the Poetry Society of Virginia.

The Poet's Domain

Rabbi Israel Zoberman

Mirror's Magic

My grandma Rachel would hold
A mirror to her glowing face—
A prayer book refusing to reflect
The blemishes of a Holocaust survivor
Finding her dear ones in tear-filled
Pages she would not let go of,
Caressing letters and connecting limbs,
Breathing sacred life into shattered words
And scattered bodies finally resting whole
In affirmation of faithful mirror's blessings.

Virginia Beach

City in the making,
dipped in blue of
sky and sea,
beaches are thy glory,
golden till eternity.
Multitude of peoples
from lands remote
make their home
within thee,
blessing thy abode.
Planes above encircle
with nation's might
and glow,
freedom's call far-reaching
from these,
God's very shores.

New and published poets in or from Delaware, the District of Columbia, Maryland, Pennsylvania, Virginia, West Virginia, and North Carolina are invited to submit original unpublished poems for consideration. Any poet who has ever been published in *The Poet's Domain* may enter regardless of place of domicile as well as any member of the Poetry Society of Virginia.

This collection is theme-driven and although the theme may suggest content limitations, there are no restrictions on poetic genre or form. Poems up to 32 lines are preferred, but longer poems are always considered. Live Wire Press will offer contracts to poets whose works are accepted for publication.

The Poet's Domain is published annually in the fall. Announcements are sent electronically. Please contact Pat Adler at padler@cstone.net if you wish to be on the mailing list. However, you may visit the Live Wire Press website, www.livewirepress.net, for announcements, upcoming themes, and submission guidelines.

Live Wire Press also publishes a short story collection, *In Good Company*. Please visit the website for information and deadlines.